I0018440

Creating Web Apps with Angular: Learn to Build Dynamic Web Pages

A Step-by-Step Guide to Web Development with Angular

BOOZMAN RICHARD

BOOKER BLUNT

Table of Content

TABLE OF CONTENTS

3

INTRODUCTION

Mastering APIs: Build and Consume APIs with Python and JavaScript

APIs (Application Programming Interfaces) are at the heart of modern web development, powering everything from mobile applications to large-scale enterprise systems. Whether you're building a simple website or a complex distributed application, APIs provide a standardized way for different software systems to communicate with each other. In today's interconnected world, mastering the creation and consumption of APIs is a crucial skill for every developer.

This book, *"Mastering APIs: Build and Consume APIs with Python and JavaScript"*, is a comprehensive guide designed to teach you the ins and outs of working with APIs. Whether you're a beginner looking to understand the fundamentals of APIs, or an experienced developer seeking to deepen your knowledge and expertise, this book will equip you with the tools and techniques needed to build, integrate, and optimize APIs using two of the most popular programming languages: **Python** and **JavaScript**.

What Will You Learn?

Throughout this book, you will learn:

1. **Understanding the Basics of APIs**: We'll start by explaining what APIs are and why they're important. You'll understand the core principles that drive API development, such as HTTP methods, status codes, and response formats like JSON and XML.

2. **Building APIs**: You'll get hands-on experience with building RESTful APIs using Python (with Flask) and JavaScript (with Express). We'll guide you through setting up your development environment, defining endpoints, and creating API responses that clients can consume.

3. **Advanced API Techniques**: As you progress, you'll explore more advanced topics such as **GraphQL, WebSocket, caching**, and **API versioning**. You'll learn when and how to implement these techniques to optimize your API's performance, scalability, and flexibility.

4. **Consuming APIs**: Learn how to interact with third-party APIs like Google Maps, Twitter, and Stripe, and integrate these services into your own web applications. You'll understand how to authenticate, send requests, and handle responses from external APIs.

5. **Security and Best Practices**: We'll also cover API security, including how to authenticate users and protect your data from unauthorized access. You'll learn the importance of **rate limiting, caching, load balancing**,

and **API documentation** to ensure your API is robust, secure, and easy to use.

6. **Deploying APIs**: Finally, we'll show you how to deploy your APIs to the cloud, ensuring they're available and scalable for production environments. Whether you're deploying to **Heroku, AWS,** or **DigitalOcean**, you'll understand the steps to get your API into the hands of users.

Who This Book is For

This book is intended for developers at all levels who want to master working with APIs. If you're a beginner, you'll find simple, clear explanations and hands-on examples to help you build a solid foundation in API development. If you're an experienced developer, you'll appreciate the advanced topics and best practices that will enhance your ability to build scalable, efficient APIs.

- **Beginner Developers**: If you've just started programming, this book will guide you through the fundamental concepts of APIs and provide practical, easy-to-follow examples.
- **Intermediate Developers**: If you already have some experience with Python or JavaScript, you'll deepen your understanding of API development and expand your

knowledge to include advanced techniques like GraphQL, WebSockets, and API security.

- **Experienced Developers**: If you're already building APIs in production, you'll find valuable insights into API versioning, performance optimization, and deployment that will help you scale your applications and improve your development process.

Why APIs Matter

In today's software ecosystem, APIs are everywhere. They connect databases, web services, mobile apps, IoT devices, and more. By providing a standard interface for systems to communicate, APIs make it possible to integrate services across platforms, companies, and devices.

From streaming data in real time to allowing users to log in using their social media accounts, APIs enable rich and interactive user experiences. As applications become increasingly complex, APIs are crucial for maintaining the flexibility, scalability, and maintainability of systems.

Structure of the Book

This book is structured in a way that allows you to build your API development skills step by step:

1. **Foundations**: We'll begin by covering the basic concepts of APIs, including HTTP methods, JSON data formats, and how to create simple APIs.

2. **Building APIs**: Next, we'll dive into creating and consuming APIs using Python (Flask) and JavaScript (Express), with real-world examples to guide you.

3. **Advanced Techniques**: Once you're comfortable with the basics, we'll explore more advanced topics like GraphQL, WebSockets, API optimization, and scaling.

4. **Real-World Applications**: Finally, we'll apply your learning with a series of real-world examples, such as building a real-time chat app using WebSockets and integrating payment functionality using Stripe.

What's Next?

By the end of this book, you will have the knowledge and skills to build powerful APIs from scratch, integrate third-party services, optimize performance, and deploy APIs to the cloud. You will be prepared to tackle real-world projects and build APIs that are robust, scalable, and easy to maintain.

So, whether you're building your first API or looking to improve your existing skills, *"Mastering APIs: Build and Consume APIs with Python and JavaScript"* is the comprehensive guide you need to master API development and unlock the potential of your applications.

CHAPTER 1

INTRODUCTION TO APIS

What APIs Are and Why They Matter

An **API** (Application Programming Interface) is a set of rules that allows one piece of software or program to communicate with another. APIs define the way software components interact with each other, and they serve as bridges between different systems, allowing them to exchange data and functionality.

APIs are fundamental in the development of modern web applications, as they enable different software applications to talk to each other over the internet. For example, when you use a mobile app that shows you the weather, the app likely uses an API to request weather data from a server and displays it in your app. Without APIs, the software wouldn't be able to interact with other services or share data efficiently.

APIs matter because they:

- Allow integration between different systems (e.g., connecting a website with a payment gateway like Stripe or PayPal).

- Enable developers to build on existing platforms and services, saving time and effort (e.g., using Google Maps API for map functionality).
- Provide a standardized way for applications to interact, making it easier to scale and maintain complex systems.

Key API Concepts

Before diving into building and consuming APIs, it's important to understand the key concepts that form the foundation of API communication:

- **Request**: A request is made when a client (like a web browser or mobile app) sends information to the server. The request could be to fetch data, submit information, or perform a task.

  Key components of a request:

  o **URL (Uniform Resource Locator)**: This specifies the location of the resource on the web.
  o **HTTP Method**: Defines the action to be performed. The most common methods are:
    - GET: Retrieve data
    - POST: Submit data
    - PUT: Update existing data
    - DELETE: Remove data

- o **Headers**: These contain metadata (e.g., content type, authorization tokens).

- o **Body**: Contains the data being sent to the server (mainly used with POST and PUT requests).

- **Response**: The response is the server's reply to the client's request. It contains the requested data or an acknowledgment that an action has been performed.

Key components of a response:

- o **Status Code**: Indicates whether the request was successful or if there was an error. Common status codes include:

  - 200 OK: The request was successful.

  - 404 Not Found: The requested resource was not found.

  - 500 Internal Server Error: A server error occurred.

- o **Body**: Contains the data being sent back to the client. For example, in a weather API, the body might include JSON data with the current temperature.

- **Endpoints**: An endpoint is a specific path on a server where an API can be accessed. For example, a weather API may have an endpoint like /weather that returns weather data when queried. Each endpoint is typically designed to handle a particular type of request or action.

13

- **Headers**: Headers are used to pass additional information with both requests and responses. Headers often carry essential information like the type of content being sent, authentication tokens, or the client's language preference.

Introduction to RESTful APIs

A **RESTful API** (Representational State Transfer) is an architectural style for creating networked applications. REST is based on stateless communication and works over HTTP, making it easy for APIs to be integrated into web apps and services. RESTful APIs use standard HTTP methods (GET, POST, PUT, DELETE) to interact with resources, which are typically represented in JSON or XML format.

Key characteristics of RESTful APIs:

- **Stateless**: Each request from a client contains all the necessary information, so the server doesn't store any session data.
- **Uniform Interface**: REST APIs follow standard conventions, such as using HTTP methods and meaningful resource names (e.g., `/users` or `/products`).
- **Cacheable**: Responses can be cached to improve performance and reduce server load.

14

- **Client-Server**: The client and server are separate entities that communicate through API calls, and each can be developed independently.

RESTful APIs are widely used in modern web development because of their simplicity, scalability, and ease of integration.

Examples of Popular APIs in the Real World

Several well-known companies offer APIs that developers use to add powerful features to their applications. Here are some real-world examples:

- **Google Maps API**: This API allows developers to embed Google Maps into websites and applications. It provides features like geolocation, route planning, and location-based services. For instance, many ride-sharing apps (like Uber) use the Google Maps API for real-time navigation and mapping.
- **Twitter API**: The Twitter API allows developers to interact with Twitter's platform, enabling actions like posting tweets, reading user timelines, and analyzing trends. Many analytics tools and third-party applications rely on the Twitter API to pull data for analysis or automation.
- **Stripe API**: Stripe is a popular payment processing service. Its API enables developers to accept payments

online in various forms (credit card, bank transfer, etc.). The API allows for secure, seamless payment experiences, which is why it's widely used in e-commerce and subscription-based businesses.

- **OpenWeatherMap API**: The OpenWeatherMap API provides real-time weather data, forecasts, and historical weather data. It is used by apps to display weather forecasts or integrate weather-related functionalities, such as showing the current temperature or precipitation chances in a specific location.

These examples demonstrate how APIs enable developers to extend the functionality of their applications without building every feature from scratch. APIs make it possible to connect services, create new user experiences, and improve the scalability of applications.

In the next chapter, we will dive deeper into how to set up your environment for building and consuming APIs using Python and JavaScript.

CHAPTER 2

SETTING UP YOUR

DEVELOPMENT ENVIRONMENT

In this chapter, we will walk through the process of setting up your development environment to build and consume APIs using Python and JavaScript. You'll also learn about the tools you'll need to streamline the development process and enhance your productivity.

Python and JavaScript Setup for API Development

Before you start developing APIs, you need to ensure that both Python and JavaScript are properly set up on your machine. Below is a step-by-step guide for setting up the environment for both languages:

Setting up Python for API Development:

1. **Install** **Python**:
   To start working with Python, you'll first need to install it. Download the latest version of Python from the official website:
   https://www.python.org/downloads/ **Make sure to check**

the box "Add Python to PATH" during the installation process to ensure it's accessible from the command line.

2. **Install pip (Package Installer for Python)**: pip is the package manager for Python and is used to install libraries that will help in API development. It is typically installed along with Python, but you can check by running the following command in your terminal:

```css
pip --version
```

3. **Install Flask**: Flask is a lightweight web framework in Python that is commonly used for building APIs. To install Flask, open your terminal and run:

```nginx
pip install flask
```

4. **Verify Installation**: After installing Flask, create a simple app.py file and run it to verify that your Python setup is correct:

```python
from flask import Flask
app = Flask(__name__)
```

18

```
@app.route('/')
def hello_world():
    return 'Hello, World!'


if __name__ == '__main__':
    app.run(debug=True)
```

Now, navigate to `http://127.0.0.1:5000/` in your web browser, and you should see "Hello, World!" displayed.

Setting up JavaScript for API Development:

1. **Install   Node.js**:
   JavaScript runs on the server side using Node.js. Download and install the latest version of Node.js from: https://nodejs.org/

2. **Verify   Node.js   and   npm**:
   After installing Node.js, you can verify the installation by running the following commands in your terminal:

   ```css
   ```

   ```
   node --version
   npm --version
   ```

3. **Install   Express**:
   Express is a popular web framework for Node.js that

simplifies API development. To install Express, navigate to your project directory and run:

```
csharp
```

```
npm init -y
npm install express
```

4. **Verify** **Installation**:

After installing Express, create a simple `app.js` file and run it to verify that your Node.js setup is correct:

```
javascript
```

```javascript
const express = require('express');
const app = express();

app.get('/', (req, res) => {
    res.send('Hello, World!');
});

app.listen(3000, () => {
    console.log('Server is running on
http://localhost:3000');
});
```

Visit `http://localhost:3000` in your browser, and you should see "Hello, World!" displayed.

Introduction to IDEs and Tools Like Postman

An **IDE (Integrated Development Environment)** is a tool that provides an all-in-one platform for writing, testing, and debugging code. Popular IDEs for Python and JavaScript include:

- **VS Code (Visual Studio Code)**: A highly recommended, lightweight IDE with support for both Python and JavaScript. It comes with useful extensions like Python, JavaScript, and REST Client, making development easier.
  - Download VS Code from: https://code.visualstudio.com/
- **PyCharm**: PyCharm is a full-featured IDE specifically for Python development. It's great for debugging and managing Python projects.
  - Download PyCharm from: https://www.jetbrains.com/pycharm/
- **WebStorm**: If you're looking for an IDE tailored to JavaScript, WebStorm is a great option. It provides advanced JavaScript features and integrates well with Node.js and Express.
  - Download WebStorm from: https://www.jetbrains.com/webstorm/

Postman is another essential tool for API development. It is used to test your APIs by simulating HTTP requests and analyzing responses. Here's how Postman fits into the workflow:

- **Send   API   Requests**: Postman allows you to easily send GET, POST, PUT, and DELETE requests to your API and see the results. This makes it much easier to test your endpoints and view responses, especially before integrating them into your app.

- **Environment   Setup**: Postman also allows you to set up different environments (e.g., production, development) and manage variables like API keys, base URLs, etc.

- **Collection   of   Requests**: Postman lets you save your requests in collections, which is helpful for keeping track of API endpoints you've tested and organizing them for later use.

To get started with Postman:

1. Download   it   from: https://www.postman.com/downloads/
2. Open Postman, create a new request, and choose the HTTP method (GET, POST, etc.).
3. Enter the URL of your API endpoint and any necessary headers or body data.

22

4. Click "Send" to view the response from your API.

Installing Required Libraries (Flask for Python, Express for JavaScript)

In this section, we've already covered how to install the core libraries for building APIs in both Python (Flask) and JavaScript (Express). To reiterate:

- **Flask Installation for Python**:

```
nginx
```

```
pip install flask
```

- **Express Installation for JavaScript**:

```
nginx
```

```
npm install express
```

These libraries will form the backbone of your API development for the rest of the book, allowing you to easily build, manage, and scale APIs.

With these tools and frameworks in place, you're now ready to begin developing APIs in both Python and JavaScript. In the next chapter, we'll dive into HTTP methods and status codes, building a deeper understanding of how APIs communicate.

CHAPTER 3

HTTP BASICS FOR API COMMUNICATION

In this chapter, we will explore the foundational concepts of **HTTP (Hypertext Transfer Protocol)**, which is the protocol that governs communication between clients (like browsers or mobile apps) and servers over the web. Understanding HTTP is crucial for working with APIs, as it is the basis for how requests are made and responses are received.

Explanation of HTTP Methods: GET, POST, PUT, DELETE

When a client communicates with an API, it sends **HTTP requests** to the server. Each request uses an HTTP **method** to specify the type of action the client wants to perform on the resource. The four most commonly used HTTP methods are **GET**, **POST**, **PUT**, and **DELETE**.

- **GET**:

  The **GET** method is used to retrieve data from the server. When you use GET, you are asking the server to send you information, such as a list of users, product details, or weather data.

  o **Example**: Fetching a list of users from an API:

```
http
```

```
GET /users
```

- **POST**:

  The **POST** method is used to send data to the server to create a new resource. When you use POST, you are sending data (such as form input or JSON data) to be processed and stored by the server.

  - **Example**: Creating a new user by sending data to an API:

  ```
  http
  ```

  ```
  POST /users
  Body: { "name": "John", "email":
  "john@example.com" }
  ```

- **PUT**:

  The **PUT** method is used to update an existing resource on the server. You send data that will replace the current data of a resource. PUT typically requires the client to send the full data for the resource being updated.

  - **Example**: Updating a user's email address:

  ```
  http
  ```

  ```
  PUT /users/123
  ```

```
Body:  {  "name":  "John",  "email":
"john.new@example.com"  }
```

- **DELETE**:

    The **DELETE** method is used to remove a resource from the server. When you use DELETE, you are asking the server to delete the specified resource.

    ○ **Example**: Deleting a user from the database:

    ```
    http
    ```

    ```
    DELETE /users/123
    ```

Each of these methods corresponds to a specific type of action (retrieving, creating, updating, or deleting data), and they are the building blocks of how APIs interact with client applications.

HTTP Status Codes and What They Mean

HTTP responses come with **status codes** that indicate the result of the request. These codes are grouped into categories based on the type of response. Here are some common HTTP status codes that you'll encounter when working with APIs:

- **2xx** – **Success**:

    These codes indicate that the request was successful, and the server has processed the request as expected.

o **200 OK**: The request was successful, and the server has returned the requested data.

   ▪ Example: GET /users returns a list of users.

o **201 Created**: The request was successful, and a new resource was created.

   ▪ Example: POST /users creates a new user.

- **3xx – Redirection**: These codes indicate that further action is needed to complete the request (e.g., following a redirection).

   o **301 Moved Permanently**: The requested resource has been moved to a new URL, and future requests should use the new URL.

   o **302 Found**: The requested resource is temporarily located at a different URL.

- **4xx – Client Errors**: These codes indicate that the request was not successful due to something the client did wrong (e.g., invalid input or missing authentication).

   o **400 Bad Request**: The server could not understand the request due to invalid syntax or missing parameters.

   o **401 Unauthorized**: The client must authenticate before accessing the resource (e.g., missing or incorrect API key).

o **404 Not Found**: The requested resource could not be found on the server.

- Example: `GET /users/999` returns a 404 if there is no user with ID 999.

o **405 Method Not Allowed**: The HTTP method used is not allowed for the requested resource (e.g., using GET instead of POST).

- **5xx – Server Errors**: These codes indicate that the server encountered an error or is unable to process the request.

o **500 Internal Server Error**: An unexpected error occurred on the server, and the request could not be completed.

o **503 Service Unavailable**: The server is currently unable to handle the request, usually due to being temporarily overloaded or undergoing maintenance.

Understanding status codes helps you diagnose problems with your API requests and handle errors effectively.

Working with Headers and Body Content

In addition to HTTP methods and status codes, every HTTP request and response contains **headers** and **body content**, which provide additional information or data.

- **Headers**:

  HTTP headers are key-value pairs that provide meta-information about the request or response. Headers are crucial for controlling the behavior of requests and responses and can carry important details like content type, authorization tokens, or cache instructions.

  Common headers include:

  - **Content-Type**: Specifies the type of data being sent in the request or response (e.g., `application/json` or `text/html`).
    - Example: `Content-Type: application/json`
  - **Authorization**: Used to pass authentication credentials, such as an API key or a token.
    - Example: `Authorization: Bearer <your-token>`
  - **Accept**: Specifies the types of data the client is willing to receive from the server.
    - Example: `Accept: application/json`

- **Body**   **Content**:

  The body of a request or response carries the actual data being transmitted. For example:

o In a **POST** request, the body might contain the data for creating a new resource (e.g., a JSON object with user information).

o In a **GET** request, the body is typically empty, as the purpose is to retrieve data.

The body can contain data in various formats:

o **JSON** (JavaScript Object Notation): A lightweight, text-based format used for transmitting data between client and server.

- Example:

```json

{
   "name": "John",
   "email": "john@example.com"
}
```

o **XML** (Extensible Markup Language): Another format for representing structured data, though JSON is more commonly used today.

o **Form Data**: Data sent from forms in web pages, typically for creating or updating resources.

Example of a POST request with headers and body content:

```http
```

```
POST /users
Host: api.example.com
Content-Type: application/json
Authorization: Bearer <your-api-key>

Body:
{
   "name": "John Doe",
   "email": "john.doe@example.com"
}
```

This POST request sends a JSON object with user data, using an Authorization header with an API key for security.

With this understanding of HTTP methods, status codes, and headers, you're now equipped to start building APIs and interacting with them. In the next chapter, we will cover how to start building your own API using Flask (Python) and Express (JavaScript).

CHAPTER 4

INTRODUCTION TO JSON AND XML DATA FORMATS

In this chapter, we will explore two key data formats used for transmitting data between APIs and clients: **JSON** (JavaScript Object Notation) and **XML** (Extensible Markup Language). Understanding these formats is essential for working with APIs, as they are the primary methods for structuring and sending data.

Why JSON is the Preferred Format for APIs

JSON is the most widely used format for API communication due to several key advantages:

1. **Simplicity**:
   JSON is lightweight and easy to read, making it a preferred format for transferring data. Its syntax is similar to JavaScript objects, which makes it straightforward to parse and generate for developers.

2. **Human-Readable**:
   JSON is easy to understand at a glance, as it uses a simple key-value pair structure. This readability is especially helpful for debugging and working with APIs.

33

Example of JSON data:

```
json

{
  "name": "John",
  "email": "john@example.com",
  "age": 30
}
```

3. **Language   Support**:

   JSON is natively supported in JavaScript, making it seamless to use for web-based applications. Many other programming languages also provide libraries for working with JSON, ensuring that it is universally accessible.

4. **Performance**:

   JSON is more compact than XML, which leads to better performance when transmitting large amounts of data. JSON's minimalistic nature reduces the amount of bandwidth required, making it faster to process and transmit.

5. **Structured   Data**:

   JSON supports complex data structures, such as arrays and nested objects, which makes it ideal for representing a wide variety of data types.

For example, in an API response, you might receive data about a user, including their name, email, and a list of their posts:

json

```json
{
  "name": "John Doe",
  "email": "john.doe@example.com",
  "posts": [
    {"title": "My First Post", "content": "This is the content of my first post."},
    {"title": "Another Post", "content": "This is another post."}
  ]
}
```

6. **Standardization**:

   JSON has become the standard for APIs because of its simplicity, efficiency, and wide adoption across programming languages. Most modern web APIs default to JSON for their data format.

Understanding XML for API Data

While **XML** is less common than JSON for modern APIs, it is still used in some systems, especially in legacy systems or industries that require more complex document structures.

1. **Structure and Syntax**:
   XML uses a tree-like structure with nested elements, each defined by opening and closing tags. Unlike JSON, which uses key-value pairs, XML organizes data into elements with attributes, making it more verbose.

   Example of XML data:

   xml

   ```
   <user>
     <name>John</name>
     <email>john@example.com</email>
     <age>30</age>
   </user>
   ```

2. **Complexity**:
   XML allows for the inclusion of attributes within tags, which can be useful for describing more complex data or metadata. However, this flexibility also leads to more complexity compared to JSON.

   Example of XML with attributes:

   xml

   ```
   <post id="1" title="My First Post">
     <content>This is the content of my first post.</content>
   ```

36

```
</post>
```

3. **Verbose and Less Efficient**: XML's tag-based structure makes it more verbose than JSON. As a result, XML messages typically require more bandwidth and are slower to parse and generate.

4. **Extensibility**: XML is designed to be extensible, which means it can support a wide variety of document types and structures. This makes it suitable for applications that require detailed metadata and document markup, such as document management systems or certain financial applications.

5. **Namespaces**: XML supports the use of namespaces, which helps prevent naming conflicts when combining different XML documents or data sources. This feature can be useful in complex systems but adds to the learning curve.

Real-World Example: Parsing JSON and XML Responses

Let's now look at how to parse JSON and XML data in Python and JavaScript, as this will help you interact with APIs that return data in either format.

1. Parsing JSON in Python: Python makes it easy to work with JSON data using the built-in `json` module.

- **Example**: Parsing a JSON response in Python

```python
import json

# JSON data (as a string)
response = '{"name": "John", "email": "john@example.com", "age": 30}'

# Parse the JSON string into a Python
dictionary
data = json.loads(response)

# Accessing data
print(data["name"])   # Output: John
print(data["email"])             #     Output: john@example.com
```

- **Example**: Sending JSON data in Python

```python
import json
import requests

url = "https://api.example.com/users"

# Data to be sent in JSON format
data = {
```

```
    "name": "John",
    "email": "john@example.com",
    "age": 30
}

# Send a POST request with JSON data
response = requests.post(url, json=data)

print(response.status_code)   # Output: 201
(Created)
```

2. Parsing JSON in JavaScript: JavaScript natively supports JSON parsing through the JSON.parse() method.

- **Example**: Parsing a JSON response in JavaScript

```javascript
// JSON data (as a string)
const response = '{"name": "John", "email":
"john@example.com", "age": 30}';

// Parse the JSON string into a JavaScript
object
const data = JSON.parse(response);

// Accessing data
console.log(data.name);   // Output: John
console.log(data.email);     //    Output:
john@example.com
```

39

- **Example**: Sending JSON data in JavaScript

```javascript
const url = 'https://api.example.com/users';

const data = {
  name: 'John',
  email: 'john@example.com',
  age: 30
};

// Send a POST request with JSON data
fetch(url, {
  method: 'POST',
  headers: {
    'Content-Type': 'application/json'
  },
  body: JSON.stringify(data)
})
.then(response => response.json())
.then(data => console.log(data))
.catch(error => console.error('Error:',
error));
```

3. Parsing XML in Python: To work with XML in Python, you can use the `xml.etree.ElementTree` module.

- **Example**: Parsing an XML response in Python

```python
python

import xml.etree.ElementTree as ET

# XML data (as a string)
response = '''<user>
                <name>John</name>

<email>john@example.com</email>
                <age>30</age>
            </user>'''

# Parse the XML string
root = ET.fromstring(response)

# Accessing data
print(root.find('name').text)    # Output:
John
print(root.find('email').text)   # Output:
john@example.com
```

4. Parsing XML in JavaScript: In JavaScript, you can use the DOMParser object to parse XML.

- **Example**: Parsing an XML response in JavaScript

```javascript
javascript
```

```javascript
const               xmlString              =
'<user><name>John</name><email>john@examp
le.com</email><age>30</age></user>';

// Parse the XML string
const parser = new DOMParser();
const               xmlDoc                 =
parser.parseFromString(xmlString,
'text/xml');

// Accessing data
const                  name                =
xmlDoc.getElementsByTagName('name')[0].te
xtContent;
const                  email               =
xmlDoc.getElementsByTagName('email')[0].t
extContent;

console.log(name);    // Output: John
console.log(email);           //    Output:
john@example.com
```

With a solid understanding of JSON and XML, you are now prepared to handle data from APIs in both formats. In the next chapter, we will focus on building and consuming your first API with Python and JavaScript, utilizing the knowledge you've gained so far.

CHAPTER 5

BUILDING YOUR FIRST API IN PYTHON WITH FLASK

In this chapter, we will walk through building your very first API using the **Flask** framework in Python. Flask is a lightweight, easy-to-use framework that is perfect for creating simple web applications and APIs.

Introduction to Flask Framework

Flask is a micro-framework for Python that allows developers to create web applications quickly and with minimal code. It is called a "micro" framework because it does not come with all the built-in tools and features that larger frameworks (like Django) have. Instead, Flask gives you the flexibility to add only the components you need, which makes it perfect for building APIs.

Flask is based on the **Werkzeug** WSGI toolkit and the **Jinja2** templating engine, and it is designed to be simple and easy to extend. Flask provides tools for routing, request handling, and returning responses, making it an excellent choice for building RESTful APIs.

Setting Up Your First Flask-Based API

To get started with Flask, you first need to install it. Here's how to set up Flask for your API development:

1. **Install Flask**: You can install Flask using Python's package manager, **pip**. Open your terminal or command prompt and run the following command:

```bash
bash
```

```bash
pip install flask
```

2. **Create Your First Flask App**: Once Flask is installed, you can start building your API. For your first API, let's create a simple API that returns a list of users. Create a new Python file, app.py, and add the following code:

```python
python
```

```python
from flask import Flask, jsonify

app = Flask(__name__)

# Sample data: List of users
users = [
```

44

```
    {"id": 1, "name": "John Doe", "email":
"john@example.com"},
    {"id":  2,  "name":  "Jane  Smith",
"email": "jane@example.com"},
    {"id":  3,  "name":  "Alice  Johnson",
"email": "alice@example.com"}
]


# Define a route for the API
@app.route('/users', methods=['GET'])
def get_users():
    return jsonify(users)


# Run the app
if __name__ == '__main__':
    app.run(debug=True)
```

3. **Explanation of the Code**:

   o **Flask App Initialization**: `app = Flask(__name__)` initializes the Flask application.

   o **Route Definition**: `@app.route('/users', methods=['GET'])` defines the route for your API. In this case, it's the `/users` endpoint that accepts GET requests.

   o **GET Method**: The function `get_users()` returns the list of users in JSON format using Flask's `jsonify()` function. This ensures that

45

the data is properly formatted as JSON for the client to consume.

- o **Running the App**: The `app.run(debug=True)` line starts the Flask development server. The `debug=True` option enables debugging, which helps you track errors during development.

4. **Running the API**: To run your API, navigate to the directory where `app.py` is located and run the following command in the terminal:

```bash
```

```
python app.py
```

This will start the Flask server. By default, it will run on `http://127.0.0.1:5000/`.

Open a web browser or use a tool like **Postman** to test your new API. Visit the following URL:

```arduino
```

```
http://127.0.0.1:5000/users
```

You should see the following JSON response:

```json
```

```json
[
  {
    "id": 1,
    "name": "John Doe",
    "email": "john@example.com"
  },
  {
    "id": 2,
    "name": "Jane Smith",
    "email": "jane@example.com"
  },
  {
    "id": 3,
    "name": "Alice Johnson",
    "email": "alice@example.com"
  }
]
```

Example: A Simple API That Returns a List of Users

Here's a complete example of the code for a simple API that returns a list of users:

```python
python

from flask import Flask, jsonify

app = Flask(__name__)

# Sample data: List of users
```

```
users = [
    {"id": 1, "name": "John Doe", "email":
"john@example.com"},
    {"id": 2, "name": "Jane Smith", "email":
"jane@example.com"},
    {"id": 3, "name": "Alice Johnson", "email":
"alice@example.com"}
]


# Define a route for the API
@app.route('/users', methods=['GET'])
def get_users():
    return jsonify(users)


# Run the app
if __name__ == '__main__':
    app.run(debug=True)
```

This code creates a basic API that serves a list of users when a GET request is made to the /users endpoint. The data is returned in JSON format, which is the standard for API communication.

Testing the API

After running your Flask application, you can test the API using:

- **Web Browser**: Open your browser and visit http://127.0.0.1:5000/users. You should see the list of users displayed in JSON format.

- **Postman**: Use Postman to make a GET request to http://127.0.0.1:5000/users. You will receive the same JSON response.

Summary

In this chapter, we introduced you to the **Flask** framework, walked you through setting up your first Flask-based API, and built a simple API that returns a list of users in JSON format. Flask is a powerful tool for building APIs, and now that you have a basic understanding of how to use it, you can begin building more complex and interactive APIs for your web applications.

In the next chapter, we will dive deeper into handling different HTTP methods like POST, PUT, and DELETE, and learn how to manage user input and data in your API.

CHAPTER 6

BUILDING YOUR FIRST API IN JAVASCRIPT WITH EXPRESS

In this chapter, we will learn how to create an API using the **Express** framework in JavaScript. Express is a minimal and flexible Node.js web application framework that provides a robust set of features for building web and mobile applications, especially APIs.

Introduction to Express Framework

Express is one of the most popular web frameworks for Node.js. It is widely used for building APIs because of its simplicity and flexibility. Express simplifies routing, middleware handling, and request-response cycles, making it a great choice for developers who need to build fast and efficient APIs.

Some reasons why Express is commonly used for API development:

- **Minimalistic**: Express is unopinionated and allows developers to decide how to structure their applications. It provides just enough functionality to build APIs but leaves the rest up to you.

- **Middleware Support**: Express allows you to use middleware to handle requests before they reach your route handlers, which is helpful for things like authentication, logging, and error handling.
- **Routing**: Express makes it easy to define routes for handling different HTTP methods (GET, POST, PUT, DELETE) and URL patterns.

Setting Up Your First Express-Based API

To get started with Express, you'll need to set up a Node.js environment and install the Express library. Here's how you can do that:

1. **Install** **Node.js**: If you haven't already, install **Node.js** from the official website: https://nodejs.org/. This will also install **npm**, which is the package manager for Node.js.
2. **Initialize a New Node.js Project**: Open your terminal, create a new directory for your project, and run the following commands:

```bash
mkdir my-api
cd my-api
npm init -y
```

The `npm init -y` command will create a `package.json` file that manages your project dependencies.

3. **Install** **Express**:
   Install Express using npm:

   ```bash
   npm install express
   ```

4. **Create Your First Express App**:
   After installing Express, create a new JavaScript file called `app.js`. This file will contain the code for your API. Here's the basic structure of your first Express-based API:

   ```javascript
   const express = require('express');
   const app = express();

   // Sample data: List of products
   const products = [
     { id: 1, name: 'Laptop', price: 999.99 },
     { id: 2, name: 'Smartphone', price:
   799.99 },
     { id: 3, name: 'Headphones', price:
   199.99 }
   ```

```
];

// Define a route for the API
app.get('/products', (req, res) => {
  res.json(products);
});

// Start the server
app.listen(3000, () => {
  console.log('Server    is    running    on
http://localhost:3000');
});
```

Explanation of the Code:

- o **Express Initialization**: `const express =
  require('express');` imports the Express
  module, and `const app = express();` creates
  an instance of an Express application.
- o **Route Definition**: `app.get('/products',
  (req, res) => { ... });` defines a GET
  route at `/products` that returns a list of products
  in JSON format.
- o **Starting the Server**: `app.listen(3000, ()
  => { ... });` starts the server on port 3000 and
  listens for incoming requests.

5. **Run the Express App:**
To start your server, run the following command in your terminal:

```bash
node app.js
```

The server will start and listen on port 3000.

Visit `http://localhost:3000/products` in your browser, and you should see the list of products displayed as JSON:

```json
[
  {
    "id": 1,
    "name": "Laptop",
    "price": 999.99
  },
  {
    "id": 2,
    "name": "Smartphone",
    "price": 799.99
  },
  {
    "id": 3,
```

```
        "name": "Headphones",
        "price": 199.99
    }
  ]
```

Example: A Simple API that Returns Product Details

Here is the full code example for an Express-based API that returns product details:

```javascript
const express = require('express');
const app = express();

// Sample data: List of products
const products = [
  { id: 1, name: 'Laptop', price: 999.99 },
  { id: 2, name: 'Smartphone', price: 799.99 },
  { id: 3, name: 'Headphones', price: 199.99 }
];

// Define a route for the API
app.get('/products', (req, res) => {
  res.json(products);
});

// Start the server
app.listen(3000, () => {
```

```
console.log('Server      is      running      on
http://localhost:3000');
});
```

Testing the API

Once your server is running, you can test the API in a few ways:

- **Web   Browser**:
  Open your web browser and navigate to
  `http://localhost:3000/products`. You should see
  the list of products returned as JSON.

- **Postman**:
  You can also use **Postman** to test your API. Open
  Postman, create a new GET request with the URL
  `http://localhost:3000/products`, and hit **Send**.
  You should receive the JSON data in the response.

- **Command   Line   (cURL)**:
  Alternatively, you can use the `curl` command to test your
  API from the command line:

```bash
curl http://localhost:3000/products
```

Conclusion

In this chapter, we introduced the **Express** framework and walked through the steps to set up your first API using JavaScript. You created an API that returns a list of products in JSON format when a GET request is made to the `/products` endpoint. Express makes it easy to handle HTTP requests and responses, and with just a few lines of code, you were able to build a fully functional API.

In the next chapter, we will explore how to handle more HTTP methods such as POST, PUT, and DELETE, allowing us to build more dynamic and interactive APIs.

CHAPTER 7

CREATING API ENDPOINTS AND ROUTING

In this chapter, we will dive into **API routing** and **creating multiple endpoints** in both **Flask (Python)** and **Express (JavaScript)**. We will explore how to define routes in your API, handle different HTTP methods (GET, POST, PUT, DELETE), and create a **CRUD (Create, Read, Update, Delete)** API with real-world examples.

Understanding Routing in Flask and Express

Routing refers to the process of defining which function will handle a specific HTTP request for a given endpoint. An **endpoint** is simply a URL that corresponds to a specific functionality within your API.

Both **Flask** and **Express** provide simple and flexible ways to define routes for your API. Let's explore how routing works in each framework:

In Flask (Python): Flask allows you to define routes using the `@app.route()` decorator. Each route corresponds to a URL pattern and can handle specific HTTP methods like GET, POST, PUT, or DELETE.

- **Example**:

```python
python

@app.route('/users', methods=['GET'])
def get_users():
    # Logic to fetch and return users
    return jsonify(users)
```

In Express (JavaScript): In Express, you define routes using methods like `app.get()`, `app.post()`, `app.put()`, and `app.delete()`. These methods correspond to different HTTP methods and allow you to handle requests for specific routes.

- **Example**:

```javascript
javascript

app.get('/users', (req, res) => {
    // Logic to fetch and return users
    res.json(users);
});
```

Both frameworks allow for the definition of routes that correspond to specific paths in the URL and associate them with a handler function that processes requests and generates responses.

Creating Multiple Endpoints in an API

APIs often consist of multiple endpoints, each serving a different purpose. For example, a blog API might have endpoints for creating a post, viewing posts, updating posts, and deleting posts. Here's how you can define multiple endpoints in both Flask and Express.

In Flask (Python): Let's extend the example to create an API with multiple endpoints for handling blog posts. We'll create endpoints to:

- Get a list of blog posts
- Create a new blog post
- Update an existing blog post
- Delete a blog post

```python
from flask import Flask, jsonify, request

app = Flask(__name__)

# Sample data: List of blog posts
posts = [
    {"id": 1, "title": "First Post", "content":
"This is my first post."},
    {"id": 2, "title": "Another Post", "content":
"This is another post."}
```

```
]


# Endpoint to get all posts
@app.route('/posts', methods=['GET'])
def get_posts():
    return jsonify(posts)


# Endpoint to create a new post
@app.route('/posts', methods=['POST'])
def create_post():
    new_post = request.get_json()
    posts.append(new_post)
    return jsonify(new_post), 201


# Endpoint to update an existing post
@app.route('/posts/<int:id>', methods=['PUT'])
def update_post(id):
    post = next((p for p in posts if p["id"] ==
id), None)
    if post:
        post_data = request.get_json()
        post.update(post_data)
        return jsonify(post)
    else:
        return    jsonify({"error":    "Post    not
found"}), 404


# Endpoint to delete a post
```

```python
@app.route('/posts/<int:id>',
methods=['DELETE'])
def delete_post(id):
    global posts
    posts = [p for p in posts if p["id"] != id]
    return jsonify({"message": "Post deleted"}),
200


# Run the app
if __name__ == '__main__':
    app.run(debug=True)
```

- **GET /posts**: Retrieves all blog posts.
- **POST /posts**: Creates a new blog post.
- **PUT /posts/<id>**: Updates an existing blog post based on its ID.
- **DELETE /posts/<id>**: Deletes a blog post based on its ID.

In Express (JavaScript): Let's build the same CRUD API in Express. We'll handle the same operations for blog posts:

```javascript
javascript

const express = require('express');
const app = express();

// Sample data: List of blog posts
let posts = [
```

```
  { id: 1, title: 'First Post', content: 'This
is my first post.' },
  { id: 2, title: 'Another Post', content:
'This is another post.' }
];


// Middleware to parse JSON request bodies
app.use(express.json());


// Endpoint to get all posts
app.get('/posts', (req, res) => {
    res.json(posts);
});


// Endpoint to create a new post
app.post('/posts', (req, res) => {
    const newPost = req.body;
    posts.push(newPost);
    res.status(201).json(newPost);
});


// Endpoint to update an existing post
app.put('/posts/:id', (req, res) => {
    const postId = parseInt(req.params.id);
    const post = posts.find(p => p.id ===
postId);
    if (post) {
        const postData = req.body;
        Object.assign(post, postData);
```

```
        res.json(post);
    } else {
        res.status(404).json({ error: 'Post not
found' });
    }
});


// Endpoint to delete a post
app.delete('/posts/:id', (req, res) => {
    const postId = parseInt(req.params.id);
    posts = posts.filter(p => p.id !== postId);
    res.status(200).json({     message:     'Post
deleted' });
});


// Start the server
app.listen(3000, () => {
    console.log('Server     is     running     on
http://localhost:3000');
});
```

- **GET /posts**: Retrieves all blog posts.
- **POST /posts**: Creates a new blog post.
- **PUT /posts/:id**: Updates an existing blog post based on its ID.
- **DELETE /posts/:id**: Deletes a blog post based on its ID.

Real-World Example: A Blog API with CRUD Operations

The examples provided above demonstrate how to create a simple blog API that allows users to perform CRUD operations on blog posts. These operations are essential in most web applications where data needs to be created, retrieved, updated, and deleted.

1. GET Request to Retrieve All Blog Posts:

- **Flask**:
    - o Request: GET /posts
    - o Response:

        ```json
        json
        ```

        ```json
        [
          {"id": 1, "title": "First Post",
        "content": "This is my first post."},
          {"id": 2, "title": "Another Post",
        "content": "This is another post."}
        ]
        ```

- **Express**:
    - o Request: GET /posts
    - o Response:

        ```json
        json
        ```

        ```json
        [
        ```

```
    {"id": 1, "title": "First Post",
"content": "This is my first post."},
    {"id": 2, "title": "Another Post",
"content": "This is another post."}
]
```

2. POST Request to Create a New Blog Post:

- **Flask**:
  - Request: POST /posts
  - Body:

    json

    ```
    {
      "id": 3,
      "title": "New Post",
      "content": "This is a newly created
    post."
    }
    ```

- **Express**:
  - Request: POST /posts
  - Body:

    json

    ```
    {
      "id": 3,
    ```

66

```
"title": "New Post",
"content": "This is a newly created
post."
}
```

3. PUT Request to Update an Existing Blog Post:

- **Flask**:
  - Request: PUT /posts/2
  - Body:

    json

    ```
    {
      "title": "Updated Post",
      "content": "This is the updated
    content of the second post."
    }
    ```

- **Express**:
  - Request: PUT /posts/2
  - Body:

    json

    ```
    {
      "title": "Updated Post",
      "content": "This is the updated
    content of the second post."
    ```

```
}
```

4. DELETE Request to Remove a Blog Post:

- **Flask:**
    - Request: DELETE /posts/1
    - Response:

        json

        ```
        {
            "message": "Post deleted"
        }
        ```

- **Express:**
    - Request: DELETE /posts/1
    - Response:

        json

        ```
        {
            "message": "Post deleted"
        }
        ```

Conclusion

In this chapter, we learned how to create multiple endpoints in both **Flask** and **Express** for building a CRUD API. We also saw how routing works in both frameworks and how you can define different routes for handling different HTTP methods (GET,

POST, PUT, DELETE). The blog API example provides a real-world scenario of how these operations can be used to manage blog posts in a web application.

In the next chapter, we will explore how to handle authentication and security in your API to ensure that only authorized users can access or modify data.

CHAPTER 8

WORKING WITH QUERY PARAMETERS AND PATH VARIABLES

In this chapter, we will explore how to use **query parameters** and **path variables** in your API to make your endpoints more dynamic and flexible. Query parameters and path variables are commonly used to filter data, pass information, and access specific resources in an API.

Understanding Query Strings and Path Parameters

1. **Query** **Parameters**:
   Query parameters are part of the URL and come after the ? symbol. They allow you to send data as key-value pairs to filter or modify the response from the server. Multiple query parameters can be separated by an & symbol.

   o **Structure**:
   ```
   http://example.com/products?categor
   y=laptop&price=1000
   ```
   - `category=laptop` and `price=1000` are the query parameters.

o **Purpose**:

Query parameters are often used for:

- Filtering data (e.g., showing products from a specific category).
- Sorting data (e.g., sorting products by price).
- Pagination (e.g., fetching only a subset of data).
- Searching (e.g., searching for products by name).

o **Example**:

A request like `GET /products?category=laptop&price=100 0` might filter a list of products to return only laptops that cost $1000.

2. **Path   Variables**:

Path variables (also called **route parameters**) are used within the URL path itself. They represent dynamic values that you can use to access specific resources.

o **Structure**:

`http://example.com/products/123`

- `123` is a path variable representing the ID of a specific product.

o **Purpose**:

Path variables are typically used when you need to access a single resource or a specific instance of a resource, such as retrieving a product by ID or updating a user profile.

- o **Example**:

  A request like `GET /products/123` might return the details of the product with ID 123.

Real-World Example: Filtering Data with Query Parameters

Let's build a real-world example of how you might use query parameters to filter data. We will extend our blog API example to allow filtering blog posts based on the **author** and **category**.

In Flask (Python):

1. **Set up a simple Flask app** with a list of blog posts.
2. **Add query parameters** to filter posts by author and category.

```python
from flask import Flask, jsonify, request

app = Flask(__name__)

# Sample data: List of blog posts
posts = [
    {"id": 1, "title": "First Post", "author":
"John Doe", "category": "Tech", "content": "This
is my first post."},
```

```
    {"id": 2, "title": "Another Post", "author":
"Jane     Smith",     "category":     "Lifestyle",
"content": "This is another post."},
    {"id": 3, "title": "Tech Post", "author":
"John Doe", "category": "Tech", "content": "This
is a tech post."}
]


# Endpoint to get filtered posts
@app.route('/posts', methods=['GET'])
def get_posts():
    # Get query parameters from the request
    author = request.args.get('author')
    category = request.args.get('category')

    # Filter posts based on query parameters
    filtered_posts = [post for post in posts if
                    (author   is   None   or
post["author"].lower() == author.lower()) and
                    (category   is   None   or
post["category"].lower() == category.lower())]

    return jsonify(filtered_posts)

# Run the app
if __name__ == '__main__':
    app.run(debug=True)
```

How it works:

- When a GET request is made to /posts, the author and category query parameters are used to filter the posts.
- For example, if you want to get all posts by "John Doe" in the "Tech" category, you can make the request:

```bash
bash
```

```
GET /posts?author=John%20Doe&category=Tech
```

In Express (JavaScript):

```javascript
javascript
```

```
const express = require('express');
const app = express();

// Sample data: List of blog posts
let posts = [
  { id: 1, title: 'First Post', author: 'John
Doe', category: 'Tech', content: 'This is my
first post.' },
  { id: 2, title: 'Another Post', author: 'Jane
Smith', category: 'Lifestyle', content: 'This is
another post.' },
  { id: 3, title: 'Tech Post', author: 'John
Doe', category: 'Tech', content: 'This is a tech
post.' }
];
```

```
// Endpoint to get filtered posts
app.get('/posts', (req, res) => {
  const { author, category } = req.query;

  // Filter posts based on query parameters
  const filteredPosts = posts.filter(post => {
    return (
      (!author || post.author.toLowerCase() ===
author.toLowerCase()) &&
      (!category || post.category.toLowerCase()
=== category.toLowerCase())
    );
  });

  res.json(filteredPosts);
});

// Start the server
app.listen(3000, () => {
  console.log('Server      is      running      on
http://localhost:3000');
});
```

How it works:

- Similar to Flask, when a GET request is made to /posts, the author and category query parameters are used to filter the posts.
- Example request:

75

```bash
bash
```

```bash
GET /posts?author=John%20Doe&category=Tech
```

Using Path Variables for Dynamic Endpoints

Now, let's look at how to use **path variables** to define dynamic endpoints that fetch, update, or delete specific resources.

In Flask (Python):

We will extend the blog API to allow retrieving a specific post by ID.

```python
python
```

```python
# Endpoint to get a specific post by ID
@app.route('/posts/<int:id>', methods=['GET'])
def get_post(id):
    post = next((p for p in posts if p["id"] ==
id), None)
    if post:
        return jsonify(post)
    else:
        return jsonify({"error": "Post not
found"}), 404
```

How it works:

- The /<int:id> part of the route is a path variable that represents the ID of a specific post.
- If a GET request is made to /posts/1, it will return the details of the post with ID 1.

In Express (JavaScript):

Similarly, we can define a dynamic endpoint to retrieve a post by its ID:

javascript

```javascript
// Endpoint to get a specific post by ID
app.get('/posts/:id', (req, res) => {
  const postId = parseInt(req.params.id);
  const post = posts.find(p => p.id === postId);

  if (post) {
    res.json(post);
  } else {
    res.status(404).json({ error: 'Post not
found' });
  }
});
```

How it works:

- The :id part of the route is a path variable that represents the ID of a specific post.

77

- Example request:

```bash
bash
```

```
GET /posts/2
```

Summary

In this chapter, we covered how to:

- Use **query parameters** to filter data in your API by including key-value pairs in the URL (e.g., `GET /posts?author=John%20Doe&category=Tech`).
- Use **path variables** to create dynamic endpoints that represent specific resources (e.g., `GET /posts/123`).
- We also built a simple **blog API** that demonstrates how to handle both types of parameters to filter and access specific data.

These techniques make your API more flexible and allow clients to interact with your data in a more dynamic and meaningful way.

In the next chapter, we will explore how to handle **authentication and authorization** to secure your API and ensure that only authorized users can access certain data or perform actions.

CHAPTER 9

CONSUMING APIS WITH PYTHON

In this chapter, we will explore how to **consume APIs** using Python. Specifically, we will use the `requests` library, which is a simple and popular library in Python for making HTTP requests. We'll cover how to make both **GET** and **POST** requests, and provide a real-world example of how to fetch weather data from a third-party API.

Using the `requests` Library in Python to Make API Calls

The **requests** library is one of the easiest and most widely used libraries in Python for making HTTP requests. It simplifies the process of sending HTTP requests and receiving responses, allowing you to interact with APIs with minimal effort.

To get started with the `requests` library, you first need to install it. You can install it via pip:

```bash
bash
```

```
pip install requests
```

Once installed, you can start using the `requests` library to make API calls.

Making GET Requests

A **GET** request is used to retrieve data from an API. It's the most common type of request when interacting with APIs, as it allows you to fetch information such as user details, product lists, or weather data.

Here's how you can make a GET request using Python's `requests` library:

```python
import requests

# API endpoint for fetching data
url = 'https://api.example.com/data'

# Send a GET request
response = requests.get(url)

# Check the response status
if response.status_code == 200:
    # Parse the JSON response
    data = response.json()
    print(data)
else:
```

```
print(f"Error: {response.status_code}")
```

In this example:

- **requests.get(url)** sends a GET request to the specified URL.
- The response is stored in the **response** variable.
- **response.status_code** checks if the request was successful (status code 200 means OK).
- **response.json()** parses the JSON data returned by the API.

Making POST Requests

A **POST** request is used to send data to an API, often to create or update resources. For example, you might use a POST request to create a new user or submit form data.

Here's how you can make a POST request using Python's requests library:

python

```
import requests

# API endpoint for posting data
url = 'https://api.example.com/users'

# Data to be sent in the request body
```

```python
data = {
    'name': 'John Doe',
    'email': 'john.doe@example.com'
}


# Send a POST request with JSON data
response = requests.post(url, json=data)


# Check the response status
if response.status_code == 201:
    print("User created successfully!")
else:
    print(f"Error: {response.status_code}")
```

In this example:

- **requests.post(url, json=data)** sends a POST request with the data (in JSON format) to the specified URL.

- **response.status_code == 201** checks if the resource was created successfully (status code 201 indicates resource creation).

- The response body, which could contain additional information about the created resource, can be accessed using **response.json()**.

Real-World Example: Fetching Weather Data from a Third-Party API

Let's apply the concepts we've learned so far with a real-world example. In this example, we will use the **OpenWeatherMap API**, which provides weather data for cities around the world. You'll need to sign up for a free API key to use this service.

1. **Sign up for an API key**: Go to OpenWeatherMap and sign up to get your free API key.
2. **Fetch weather data for a city**: Using the API key, we will make a GET request to fetch the current weather data for a city (e.g., New York).

Here's how to do it:

```python
import requests

# OpenWeatherMap API URL and API key
api_key = 'your_api_key_here'
city = 'New York'
url = f'http://api.openweathermap.org/data/2.5/weather?q={city}&appid={api_key}'

# Send a GET request to the API
response = requests.get(url)
```

```
# Check if the request was successful
if response.status_code == 200:
    # Parse the JSON response
    data = response.json()

    # Extract specific data from the response
    city_name = data['name']
    weather_description                          =
data['weather'][0]['description']
    temperature = data['main']['temp'] - 273.15
# Convert from Kelvin to Celsius

    # Display the weather data
    print(f"Weather       in        {city_name}:
{weather_description}")
    print(f"Temperature: {temperature:.2f}°C")
else:
    print(f"Error: {response.status_code}")
```

How it works:

- **API URL**: The URL for the OpenWeatherMap API contains the city name and the API key. We dynamically build the URL by inserting the city name and the API key.
- **GET request**: We send a GET request to the URL to fetch the weather data.

- **Parsing the response**: The response is returned as a JSON object, which we can parse using `response.json()`.

- **Extracting specific data**: We extract the relevant data from the JSON response, such as the city name, weather description, and temperature. Note that the temperature is returned in Kelvin, so we convert it to Celsius by subtracting 273.15.

- **Displaying the result**: The weather description and temperature are printed out in a user-friendly format.

Example output:

```vbnet
Weather in New York: clear sky
Temperature: 22.35°C
```

Summary

In this chapter, we covered how to use Python's **requests** library to consume APIs. We learned how to make **GET** and **POST** requests, and how to handle responses from the server. We also explored a real-world example of fetching weather data from the **OpenWeatherMap API**.

By now, you should be comfortable making API calls with Python, extracting useful data, and displaying it in your application. In the next chapter, we will dive deeper into handling

errors in API requests and responses, and how to improve your code's robustness when interacting with third-party APIs.

CHAPTER 10

CONSUMING APIS WITH JAVASCRIPT

In this chapter, we will explore how to consume APIs using **JavaScript**. We will focus on two popular methods for making HTTP requests: **fetch** and **axios**. These tools allow us to interact with APIs by sending GET and POST requests, and we will also walk through a real-world example of fetching user data from a REST API.

Using fetch and axios to Make API Calls

JavaScript provides two primary ways to make HTTP requests to interact with APIs:

1. **fetch API**: The fetch API is a modern, built-in JavaScript method that makes HTTP requests. It is promise-based, which means it allows asynchronous requests and is widely supported in modern browsers.

   Basic Usage of fetch:

   ```javascript
   ```

   ```
   fetch('https://api.example.com/data')
   ```

```
.then(response => response.json())   //
Parse the JSON response
.then(data => console.log(data))     //
Use the data
.catch(error => console.error('Error:',
error));  // Handle errors
```

- o fetch returns a **promise** that resolves to the response of the request.
- o We use .then(response => response.json()) to parse the JSON data from the response.
- o .catch(error => console.error(...)) handles any errors that occur during the request.

2. **axios Library**: **Axios** is a popular third-party library for making HTTP requests in JavaScript. It simplifies the process of making requests and has some advantages over fetch, such as automatic JSON parsing and easier error handling.

Installing axios: If you're using a package manager like npm or yarn, you can install **axios**:

```bash
bash
```

```
npm install axios
```

Basic Usage of axios:

```javascript

const axios = require('axios');  // Import axios

axios.get('https://api.example.com/data')
  .then(response =>
console.log(response.data))    // Use the data from the response
  .catch(error => console.error('Error:', error));  // Handle errors
```

- o axios.get sends a GET request and returns a promise.
- o The response is automatically parsed, so we can directly access response.data.
- o Like fetch, axios also provides .then() and .catch() for handling the response and errors.

Both fetch and axios can be used for making API requests. axios has a more user-friendly syntax, but fetch is built into modern browsers and does not require additional dependencies.

Making GET and POST Requests in JavaScript

1. **GET Request with fetch**: A **GET** request is used to retrieve data from an API. Here's how you can use fetch to make a GET request in JavaScript:

```javascript
fetch('https://jsonplaceholder.typicode.com/users')
  .then(response => response.json())
  .then(data => console.log(data))
  .catch(error => console.error('Error:', error));
```

In this example:

- o We're fetching a list of users from the `jsonplaceholder` API, which is a free fake API used for testing.
- o The response is parsed as JSON using `response.json()`.
- o The result is logged to the console.

2. **POST Request with `fetch`**: A **POST** request is used to send data to the server. Here's how you can send a POST request with JSON data:

```javascript
const newUser = {
  name: 'John Doe',
  email: 'john.doe@example.com'
};
```

```
fetch('https://jsonplaceholder.typicode.c
om/users', {
  method: 'POST',
  headers: {
    'Content-Type': 'application/json'
  },
  body: JSON.stringify(newUser)
})
.then(response => response.json())
.then(data => console.log('User created:',
data))
.catch(error   =>   console.error('Error:',
error));
```

In this example:

- o We're sending data (new user details) to the API.
- o The method: 'POST' option specifies that we are making a POST request.
- o The headers indicate that we are sending JSON data.
- o The body: JSON.stringify(newUser) serializes the data before sending it to the server.
- o The response is parsed as JSON, and the created user's data is logged.

3. **GET Request with axios**: Using axios, the syntax for making a GET request is quite similar:

```
javascript
```

```javascript
axios.get('https://jsonplaceholder.typico
de.com/users')
  .then(response                     =>
console.log(response.data))
  .catch(error => console.error('Error:',
error));
```

- o The response data is directly available through response.data (no need for .json() like in fetch).

4. **POST Request with axios**: Making a POST request with axios is even simpler:

```
javascript
```

```javascript
const newUser = {
  name: 'John Doe',
  email: 'john.doe@example.com'
};

axios.post('https://jsonplaceholder.typic
ode.com/users', newUser)
  .then(response    =>    console.log('User
created:', response.data))
  .catch(error => console.error('Error:',
error));
```

- The `axios.post` method automatically sends the data as JSON.
- The response data is available through `response.data`.

Real-World Example: Fetching User Data from a REST API

Let's consider a real-world example of fetching user data from a **REST API** using both `fetch` and `axios`.

We will fetch the list of users from the **JSONPlaceholder API** (a free REST API for testing). Here's how you would use both `fetch` and `axios` to get the list of users.

Using `fetch`:

javascript

```
// Fetch user data with fetch API
fetch('https://jsonplaceholder.typicode.com/use
rs')
  .then(response => response.json())  // Parse
JSON response
  .then(users => {
    console.log('Users  fetched  with  fetch:',
users);
  })
  .catch(error => {
```

```
      console.error('Error  fetching  data  with
fetch:', error);
  });
```

Using axios:

```javascript
const axios = require('axios');

// Fetch user data with axios
axios.get('https://jsonplaceholder.typicode.com
/users')
  .then(response => {
    console.log('Users  fetched  with  axios:',
response.data);
  })
  .catch(error => {
    console.error('Error  fetching  data  with
axios:', error);
  });
```

Both methods will fetch a list of users from the jsonplaceholder **API** and print them to the console. The fetch method requires parsing the response as JSON, whereas axios automatically parses the response for you, making it slightly more convenient.

Sample Output:

json

```
[
  {
    "id": 1,
    "name": "Leanne Graham",
    "username": "Bret",
    "email": "Sincere@april.biz",
    "address": {
      "street": "Kulas Light",
      "suite": "Apt. 556",
      "city": "Gwenborough",
      "zipcode": "92998-3874",
      "geo": {
        "lat": "-37.3159",
        "lng": "81.1496"
      }
    },
    "phone": "1-770-736-8031 x56442",
    "website": "hildegard.org",
    "company": {
      "name": "Romaguera-Crona",
      "catchPhrase":    "Multi-layered    client-
server neural-net",
      "bs": "harness real-time e-markets"
    }
  },
  ...
]
```

This is just an example of the response you would get, which includes user data such as `name`, `email`, `address`, and more.

Summary

In this chapter, we covered how to consume APIs in JavaScript using the **fetch** and **axios** methods. Both tools allow you to interact with external APIs by sending **GET** and **POST** requests. We provided real-world examples of fetching user data from a REST API, using both `fetch` and `axios`, and demonstrated how each method works with JavaScript promises.

You should now be comfortable with fetching data from APIs, sending data to APIs, and handling responses in a way that suits your needs. In the next chapter, we will dive into handling **error responses** and managing **API rate limits**.

CHAPTER 11

AUTHENTICATION AND AUTHORIZATION

In this chapter, we will dive into **API security** and explore how to ensure that only authorized users can access certain API endpoints or perform specific actions. We will cover the concepts of **authentication** and **authorization**, and explain how technologies like **OAuth 2.0** and **API keys** are commonly used to secure APIs.

Overview of API Security

API security is crucial for protecting sensitive data and ensuring that only legitimate users and systems can interact with your API. Without proper security measures, an API can be vulnerable to unauthorized access, data breaches, or malicious activities.

There are two primary concepts in API security:

1. **Authentication**:
   Authentication verifies the identity of the user or system making the request. The goal is to ensure that the person or system interacting with your API is who they claim to be.

97

Common authentication methods include:

- o **Basic Authentication**: The client sends a username and password in the request header (often base64-encoded).
- o **Bearer Tokens**: A token (usually a long string) is used to authenticate the client, often included in the request headers.
- o **OAuth 2.0**: A more secure and flexible method that allows users to grant third-party applications limited access to their resources without sharing their credentials.

2. **Authorization**:

Authorization determines what actions a user or system is allowed to perform once authenticated. It defines the permissions granted to authenticated users, such as read, write, or delete access.

Authorization often involves:

- o **Roles**: Assigning roles (e.g., Admin, User) to authenticated users.
- o **Scopes**: Restricting access to specific resources or actions based on the user's role or permissions.

Together, **authentication** and **authorization** ensure that your API is secure, and that only the right people or systems can perform the right actions.

Understanding OAuth and API Keys

1. **OAuth 2.0**:

   OAuth 2.0 is a popular authorization framework that allows third-party applications to access a user's resources without requiring the user to share their credentials. OAuth 2.0 is widely used for securing APIs and provides a way to delegate access to APIs through **access tokens**.

   How OAuth 2.0 Works:

   o **Authorization Server**: The server that issues access tokens after authenticating the user.

   o **Resource Server**: The API server that hosts the resources (e.g., Google API, GitHub API).

   o **Access Token**: A token that is issued by the authorization server, and is used by the client to access resources on the resource server. It has an expiration time and can be restricted to specific actions (e.g., read or write).

   o **Scopes**: OAuth allows the user to specify what level of access the client should have. For example, a user can allow a third-party application to access their profile data but not their email.

Flow of OAuth 2.0:

o The user is redirected to the authorization server to log in and grant permission to the third-party application.

o After granting permission, the authorization server sends an authorization code to the client.

o The client exchanges the authorization code for an access token, which is used to authenticate API requests.

OAuth 2.0 is widely used in modern APIs because it allows users to authenticate via services like **Google**, **Facebook**, **Twitter**, and others, without having to share their passwords directly.

2. **API Keys**:

An **API key** is a unique identifier used to authenticate a client to an API. The client includes the API key in the request (usually in the headers or URL) to prove their identity to the API.

API keys are simpler to implement compared to OAuth but are less secure because they don't provide a way to scope permissions or revoke access easily. They are typically used for:

- o Public APIs that don't require complex access control.
- o Rate-limiting and tracking usage of an API.

Example of an API Key:

- o URL:

```
https://api.example.com/data?api_ke
y=your-api-key-here
```

API keys are less secure than OAuth because they are static and can be exposed in requests. However, for many APIs, especially those that don't handle sensitive user data, API keys are a quick and easy method for basic security.

Real-World Example: Integrating OAuth 2.0 with Google APIs

In this example, we will use **OAuth 2.0** to authenticate and authorize access to Google's APIs. We will walk through the steps for authenticating a user via OAuth 2.0, and accessing Google's **Google Sheets API** to retrieve data from a Google Sheet.

1. Set Up a Google Cloud Project:

To use Google APIs, you need to create a project in the **Google Cloud Console** and enable the relevant API (in this case, the **Google Sheets API**).

- Go to Google Cloud Console.
- Create a new project.
- Enable the **Google Sheets API** under the "APIs & Services" section.
- Go to **Credentials**, and create **OAuth 2.0 credentials**.
- Download the **credentials JSON** file, which will contain your **Client ID** and **Client Secret**.

2. Install Required Libraries:

You'll need to install the `google-auth` and `google-auth-oauthlib` libraries to handle OAuth 2.0 authentication.

```bash

pip install google-auth google-auth-oauthlib google-auth-httplib2 google-api-python-client
```

3. Authenticate Using OAuth 2.0:

Here is a Python example using OAuth 2.0 to authenticate the user and access the Google Sheets API:

```python

```

```python
import os
import pickle
import google_auth_oauthlib.flow
from googleapiclient.discovery import build
from google.auth.transport.requests import Request

# Path to the credentials file you downloaded
from Google Cloud Console
CLIENT_SECRET_FILE = 'path_to_credentials.json'
API_NAME = 'sheets'
API_VERSION = 'v4'
SCOPES = ['https://www.googleapis.com/auth/spreadsheets.readonly']

def authenticate_google_api():
    """Authenticate the user and create a service object."""
    creds = None
    # Check if token.pickle exists (this stores the user's access and refresh tokens)
    if os.path.exists('token.pickle'):
        with open('token.pickle', 'rb') as token:
            creds = pickle.load(token)

    # If there's no valid credentials available, let the user log in.
```

```
    if not creds or not creds.valid:
        if   creds   and   creds.expired   and
creds.refresh_token:
            creds.refresh(Request())
        else:
            flow                          =
google_auth_oauthlib.flow.InstalledAppFlow.from
_client_secrets_file(
                CLIENT_SECRET_FILE, SCOPES)
            creds                         =
flow.run_local_server(port=0)

        # Save the credentials for the next run
        with   open('token.pickle',   'wb')   as
token:
            pickle.dump(creds, token)

    # Build the service object for Google Sheets
API
    service   =   build(API_NAME,   API_VERSION,
credentials=creds)
    return service

def get_google_sheet_data():
    """Fetch   data   from   a   specific   Google
Sheet."""
    service = authenticate_google_api()
```

```
    # The ID and range of the spreadsheet to
access
    SPREADSHEET_ID = 'your-spreadsheet-id-here'
    RANGE_NAME = 'Sheet1!A1:C10'    # Adjust the
range as needed

    # Call the Sheets API
    sheet = service.spreadsheets()
    result                                    =
sheet.values().get(spreadsheetId=SPREADSHEET_ID
, range=RANGE_NAME).execute()
    rows = result.get('values', [])

    if not rows:
        print('No data found.')
    else:
        for row in rows:
            print(row)

# Call the function to fetch data from the Google
Sheet
get_google_sheet_data()
```

How it works:

- **OAuth 2.0 Authentication**: The script uses OAuth 2.0 to authenticate the user. It saves the credentials to a file (token.pickle) for future use, so the user won't need to authenticate every time.

105

- **Accessing the API**: The script builds a Google Sheets API client and uses it to fetch data from a specific sheet using its ID and a range (e.g., `Sheet1!A1:C10`).
- **Displaying Data**: If the data is successfully retrieved, it is printed to the console.

4. Run the Application:

- Run the script, and you will be prompted to log in with your Google account.
- After logging in and granting permission to access your Google Sheets, the data from the specified range will be printed.

Summary

In this chapter, we learned about **API security**, including **authentication** and **authorization**, and how to secure APIs using methods like **OAuth 2.0** and **API keys**. We also went through a **real-world example** of integrating **OAuth 2.0** with **Google APIs** (Google Sheets) to authenticate a user and retrieve data from a Google Sheet.

By implementing OAuth 2.0, you can securely allow users to authenticate and access resources on their behalf without sharing their credentials. This chapter laid the foundation for integrating APIs with strong authentication mechanisms, and in the next chapter, we will discuss **error handling** in APIs to make your application more resilient and user-friendly.

CHAPTER 12

HANDLING ERRORS IN APIS

In this chapter, we will discuss **error handling** in APIs, which is a critical part of building robust and user-friendly applications. We'll explore **common API errors**, how to use **HTTP status codes** to represent errors, and how to implement **custom error messages**. We will also look at real-world examples of error handling in **Flask** (Python) and **Express** (JavaScript) APIs.

Common API Errors and How to Handle Them

When building an API, it is essential to anticipate errors and provide useful feedback to users or clients consuming your API. Common errors include:

1. **Client Errors (4xx Status Codes)**: These errors occur when the client makes an invalid request. They are typically caused by missing or incorrect parameters, invalid authentication, or not following the expected request format.

   o **400 Bad Request**: The server cannot process the request due to invalid input (e.g., missing required parameters).

- o **401 Unauthorized**: The client is not authorized to access the resource (e.g., missing or invalid API key or token).

- o **403 Forbidden**: The client is authenticated but does not have permission to perform the action.

- o **404 Not Found**: The requested resource does not exist on the server.

- o **405 Method Not Allowed**: The HTTP method used (GET, POST, etc.) is not supported for the requested resource.

2. **Server Errors (5xx Status Codes)**: These errors occur when something goes wrong on the server side, preventing the server from processing the request. These errors are often related to issues with the server, database, or application logic.

- o **500 Internal Server Error**: A general error indicating that something went wrong on the server side.

- o **502 Bad Gateway**: The server is acting as a gateway or proxy and received an invalid response from the upstream server.

- o **503 Service Unavailable**: The server is temporarily unavailable, usually due to maintenance or high traffic.

3. **Validation Errors**: These errors occur when the data provided by the client

doesn't meet the required format or constraints. For example, if a required field is missing or an email address doesn't have the correct format.

4. **Timeout** **Errors**: These errors happen when the server takes too long to respond, and the request times out. This can occur if the server is overloaded or if the client's connection is unstable.

HTTP Status Codes and Custom Error Messages

HTTP status codes play a significant role in API error handling because they provide a standardized way to communicate the success or failure of a request. It is important to use the correct status code to reflect the nature of the error.

Here's a breakdown of common HTTP status codes and how to handle them:

- **200 OK**: Indicates a successful request. Always use this for successful responses.
- **201 Created**: Indicates that a resource was successfully created (usually used for POST requests).
- **400 Bad Request**: Use this when the client sends invalid data or the request cannot be processed.

- **401 Unauthorized**: This status code is used when authentication is required and has failed or has not yet been provided.
- **404 Not Found**: Use this when the requested resource cannot be found.
- **500 Internal Server Error**: Use this when something goes wrong on the server side.

Custom Error Messages: You can provide more detailed error information by sending custom error messages in the response body. These messages help the client understand why the request failed and what they can do to fix it.

Example of a Custom Error Message:

```json

{
  "error": "Invalid data",
  "message": "The 'email' field is required."
}
```

When designing error responses, it's essential to:

- Provide a **clear** and **useful** error message.
- Include **additional details** when necessary (e.g., validation errors, missing fields).

- Return a **specific status code** that indicates the nature of the problem.

Real-World Example: Implementing Error Handling in Flask and Express APIs

In Flask (Python): Flask provides a straightforward way to handle errors using **try-except** blocks and Flask's **abort()** function. Here's how you can implement error handling for common scenarios in Flask.

python

```
from flask import Flask, jsonify, request, abort

app = Flask(__name__)

# Sample data: List of users
users = [
    {"id": 1, "name": "John Doe", "email":
"john@example.com"},
    {"id": 2, "name": "Jane Smith", "email":
"jane@example.com"}
]

# Endpoint to get a specific user by ID
@app.route('/users/<int:id>', methods=['GET'])
def get_user(id):
```

```
    user = next((u for u in users if u["id"] ==
id), None)
        if user is None:
            # Return a 404 error if user is not found
            abort(404, description="User not found")
        return jsonify(user)


# Error handling for 404 errors
@app.errorhandler(404)
def not_found_error(error):
    return    jsonify({"error":    "Not    Found",
"message": error.description}), 404


# Error handling for 400 errors
@app.errorhandler(400)
def bad_request_error(error):
    return    jsonify({"error":    "Bad    Request",
"message": "Invalid request format"}), 400


# Run the app
if __name__ == '__main__':
    app.run(debug=True)
```

How it works:

- If a user is not found, we use abort(404, description="User not found") to raise a 404 Not Found error.

113

- We define custom error handlers for 404 and 400 errors. When an error occurs, Flask automatically calls the appropriate handler and returns a custom error message in JSON format.

In Express (JavaScript): Express has built-in error handling middleware that allows you to catch errors and return appropriate responses.

```javascript
const express = require('express');
const app = express();

// Sample data: List of users
let users = [
    { id: 1, name: 'John Doe', email: 'john@example.com' },
    { id: 2, name: 'Jane Smith', email: 'jane@example.com' }
];

// Endpoint to get a specific user by ID
app.get('/users/:id', (req, res, next) => {
  const userId = parseInt(req.params.id);
  const user = users.find(u => u.id === userId);

  if (!user) {
    // Return a 404 error if user is not found
```

114

```
    const error = new Error('User not found');
    error.status = 404;
    return next(error);
  }

  res.json(user);
});


// Error handling middleware
app.use((err, req, res, next) => {
  const statusCode = err.status || 500;
  const message = err.message || 'Internal Server
Error';
  res.status(statusCode).json({ error: message
});
});


// Start the server
app.listen(3000, () => {
  console.log('Server    is    running    on
http://localhost:3000');
});
```

How it works:

- If a user is not found, we create a custom error with a message and a status code of 404 and pass it to the next middleware using next(error).

115

- The error-handling middleware catches the error and sends a custom response with the appropriate status code and message.

Example Error Responses

Flask (Python):

```json
{
  "error": "Not Found",
  "message": "User not found"
}
```

Express (JavaScript):

```json
{
  "error": "User not found"
}
```

Summary

In this chapter, we explored **error handling** in APIs, focusing on how to use **HTTP status codes** and **custom error messages** to communicate errors to the client. We discussed common API errors (e.g., 400 Bad Request, 404 Not Found, 500 Internal Server Error) and how to handle them in **Flask** and **Express** APIs. By properly handling errors, you can provide meaningful feedback to users and ensure a smoother experience when interacting with your API.

In the next chapter, we will look into **pagination and rate limiting** to manage large amounts of data and prevent overuse of your API.

CHAPTER 13

WORKING WITH API RATE LIMITING

In this chapter, we will explore **API rate limiting**, a crucial concept for controlling the number of requests made to an API within a certain time period. Rate limiting helps maintain the stability, performance, and security of an API by preventing misuse or overuse of resources. We will cover what rate limiting is, why it's important, how to implement it in your APIs, and how to handle rate limiting when consuming third-party APIs.

What is Rate Limiting and Why It's Important

Rate limiting is a technique used by API providers to limit the number of API requests that can be made by a user or application within a specific time window. This ensures that a single user or client cannot overwhelm the server by sending too many requests in a short period of time.

- **Why is rate limiting important?**
  - o **Prevent Abuse**: Rate limiting protects the API from misuse or malicious attacks, such as **Denial of Service (DoS)** attacks, where an attacker tries to overload the server with too many requests.

118

- o **Fair Usage**: It ensures that all users of the API have a fair chance to access resources without any one user consuming all the server's resources.

- o **Protect Resources**: Some operations in an API may consume a lot of computational power or bandwidth. By limiting the number of requests, you prevent overuse of these valuable resources.

- o **Server Load Management**: Rate limiting helps manage the load on the server by ensuring that requests are spaced out and that the server doesn't become overloaded.

- o **Cost Control**: For APIs that charge based on usage (such as cloud-based services), rate limiting can help control costs by limiting the number of calls made by each client.

Implementing Rate Limiting in Your APIs

There are different approaches to rate limiting, but the basic principle is to define a limit on the number of requests that can be made within a given time period (e.g., 100 requests per minute). When the limit is exceeded, the server will respond with an error, typically **HTTP 429 Too Many Requests**.

1. **Basic Rate Limiting**: You can implement simple rate limiting by tracking the number of requests made by a user (or IP address) within a time window. Once the limit

is reached, the user is temporarily blocked from making further requests.

2. **Sliding Window Rate Limiting**: This method tracks requests over a sliding window, such as the last 60 seconds, and allows a fixed number of requests within that time frame. This approach provides more flexibility and allows requests to be distributed evenly over time.

3. **Token Bucket and Leaky Bucket Algorithms**: These are more advanced algorithms used for rate limiting that offer a balance between strict rate limiting and smooth request flow. These algorithms are especially useful when you need more complex rate-limiting behavior, such as allowing bursts of traffic while still enforcing an overall limit.

4. **Implementing Rate Limiting in Flask**: In Flask, you can implement basic rate limiting using libraries like `Flask-Limiter`. Here's how to use it to limit the number of requests a user can make to an API.

Install Flask-Limiter:

bash

```
pip install Flask-Limiter
```

Example: Rate Limiting in Flask:

python

```
from flask import Flask, jsonify
from flask_limiter import Limiter
from        flask_limiter.util        import
get_remote_address

app = Flask(__name__)
limiter             =             Limiter(app,
key_func=get_remote_address)

# Set rate limit: 5 requests per minute per
IP address
@app.route('/api/data')
@limiter.limit("5 per minute")
def get_data():
    return    jsonify({"message":    "Data
fetched successfully!"})

if __name__ == '__main__':
    app.run(debug=True)
```

Explanation:

- o   We use the `Flask-Limiter` library to apply rate limiting to the `/api/data` endpoint.

- o   The `@limiter.limit("5 per minute")` decorator ensures that each user (identified by their IP address) can only access this endpoint 5 times per minute.

121

o   If the user exceeds this limit, they will receive an HTTP 429 status code with a message indicating that they have exceeded the rate limit.

5. **Implementing Rate Limiting in Express**: In **Express**, you can use middleware like `express-rate-limit` to apply rate limiting to your API.

Install express-rate-limit:

bash

```bash
npm install express-rate-limit
```

Example: Rate Limiting in Express:

javascript

```javascript
const express = require('express');
const rateLimit = require('express-rate-limit');
const app = express();

// Create a rate limit rule: 5 requests per minute
const limiter = rateLimit({
  windowMs: 60 * 1000, // 1 minute
  max: 5, // limit each IP to 5 requests per windowMs
```

```
    message: "Too many requests, please try
again later."
});

// Apply the rate limit to all API routes
app.use('/api', limiter);

app.get('/api/data', (req, res) => {
  res.json({   message:   "Data   fetched
successfully!" });
});

app.listen(3000, () => {
  console.log('Server   is   running   on
http://localhost:3000');
});
```

Explanation:

- o   express-rate-limit is used to limit requests to 5 per minute per IP address.
- o   The limiter middleware is applied to all routes under /api, so any request to /api/data will be rate-limited.
- o   If a client exceeds the limit, they will receive a 429 status code with a custom message.

Real-World Example: Handling Rate Limiting with Third-Party APIs like Twitter

When consuming third-party APIs, you often encounter rate limits that restrict the number of requests you can make in a specific time period. For instance, **Twitter's API** has rate limits that define how many requests you can make within a 15-minute window.

Example: Handling Rate Limiting with Twitter API:

Assuming you are interacting with the Twitter API, you can handle rate limiting by checking the **rate limit headers** in the API response. Twitter returns rate limit information in the headers of each response, including:

- **X-RateLimit-Limit**: The maximum number of requests that can be made in the current window.
- **X-RateLimit-Remaining**: The number of requests remaining in the current window.
- **X-RateLimit-Reset**: The time when the rate limit will reset (in UNIX timestamp format).

Here's an example of how to check for rate limits when making requests to the Twitter API using **axios** in JavaScript:

```javascript
const axios = require('axios');
```

```
const              twitterApiUrl           =
'https://api.twitter.com/2/tweets';
const accessToken = 'YOUR_TWITTER_BEARER_TOKEN';

axios.get(twitterApiUrl, {
  headers: {
    'Authorization': `Bearer ${accessToken}`
  }
})
.then(response => {
  console.log('Tweets:', response.data);

  // Check rate limit headers
  const limit = response.headers['x-ratelimit-
limit'];
  const   remaining   =   response.headers['x-
ratelimit-remaining'];
  const   resetTime   =   response.headers['x-
ratelimit-reset'];

  console.log(`Rate limit: ${remaining}/${limit}
requests remaining`);
  console.log(`Rate limit resets at: ${new
Date(resetTime * 1000)}`);
})
.catch(error => {
  if (error.response.status === 429) {
```

```
      console.log('Rate limit exceeded. Try again
later.');
    } else {
      console.error('Error:', error);
    }
});
```

How it works:

- The API call is made to the Twitter endpoint using **axios**.
- After the request is completed, we check the rate limit headers to see how many requests are left and when the limit will reset.
- If the rate limit is exceeded (HTTP status 429), the client is informed to try again later.

Summary

In this chapter, we explored the concept of **API rate limiting** and why it is essential for maintaining fair usage, preventing abuse, and protecting server resources. We learned how to implement rate limiting in APIs using both **Flask** (Python) and **Express** (JavaScript) and saw how to handle rate limits when consuming third-party APIs like Twitter. By implementing rate limiting, you can ensure that your API remains stable, efficient, and secure.

In the next chapter, we will discuss **pagination** in APIs, helping you manage large datasets and provide more efficient ways of retrieving information.

CHAPTER 14

CACHING IN API DEVELOPMENT

In this chapter, we will explore **caching**, a technique used to improve the performance of APIs by temporarily storing frequently accessed data. Caching can help reduce response times, minimize server load, and improve the scalability of your API. We will discuss the basics of caching, its benefits, common techniques, and how to implement caching with **Redis**.

What is Caching and How Does it Improve Performance?

Caching is the process of storing copies of frequently accessed data in a temporary storage area, known as a cache, so that subsequent requests for the same data can be served faster without needing to retrieve the data from the source (e.g., a database or external API). Caching can be applied to various layers of the application, including the application layer, database layer, and HTTP layer.

How Caching Improves Performance:

- **Reduced Latency**: By storing data in a cache, the time it takes to retrieve the data is significantly reduced, as cache access is much faster than database queries or external API calls.

- **Reduced Server Load**: Caching minimizes the number of requests that hit the server or database, helping to distribute the load more efficiently and preventing the server from being overwhelmed.

- **Faster Responses**: Caching allows you to serve data from memory or other fast storage systems instead of querying slower databases or external services, resulting in faster response times.

- **Cost Reduction**: For APIs that call external services or databases, caching reduces the frequency of expensive operations, helping to reduce costs associated with API calls, network bandwidth, or database queries.

Common Caching Scenarios:

- Storing frequently accessed data like product listings or user profiles.
- Caching the results of complex computations or database queries.
- Caching responses from external APIs to avoid redundant calls (e.g., weather data or financial data).

Techniques for Caching API Responses

There are various techniques for caching data in an API. Let's explore some of the most common ones:

1. **In-Memory Caching**: In-memory caching stores data in the server's memory (RAM). Since accessing data from memory is extremely fast, this is one of the most common caching methods for improving API performance.

   o **Examples**:

      ▪ Using **Redis** or **Memcached** to store data in memory.

      ▪ Caching individual API responses or query results.

2. **HTTP Caching**: HTTP caching is a way of telling clients (browsers, API consumers) that they can reuse previously fetched data without having to send a request to the server. HTTP headers such as `Cache-Control`, `ETag`, and `Last-Modified` help manage the cache behavior.

   o **Cache-Control**: Tells the client how long to store the data in cache (`max-age`, `no-cache`).

   o **ETag**: A unique identifier for a resource, allowing clients to check if the cached version is still valid.

   o **Last-Modified**: Indicates the last time the resource was modified, so clients can check for updates.

3. **Database Query Caching**: Query caching stores the results of frequently used database queries. This reduces the need to execute the same query repeatedly and can be particularly useful for read-heavy applications.

- o **Examples**:
  - Caching database query results using an in-memory store like Redis.
  - Database query caches within the database system itself (e.g., MySQL query cache).

4. **Distributed Caching**: Distributed caching allows you to share cached data across multiple servers or systems. This is useful when you need to scale your application across multiple machines.

- o **Examples**:
  - Using **Redis** or **Memcached** as a shared cache between multiple application servers.
  - Data is stored in a central cache that can be accessed by any server, ensuring consistency and reducing redundant data retrieval.

Real-World Example: Using Redis for Caching API Responses

Redis is a widely used in-memory data store that can be employed to cache API responses. It provides an efficient way to store and retrieve data quickly, making it ideal for caching purposes.

Steps for Implementing Caching with Redis:

1. Install Redis.
2. Install the **Redis Python client** or **Redis Node.js client**.
3. Use Redis to store frequently accessed data.

Let's walk through an example of caching API responses using Redis in both Python (Flask) and JavaScript (Express).

1. Using Redis for Caching in Flask (Python):

To get started, you need to install the **Redis** server and the `redis` Python client.

- **Install Redis**: Follow the installation instructions for Redis on your system: https://redis.io/download.
- **Install the Redis Python client**:

```bash
pip install redis
```

Here's an example of how to cache API responses using Redis in a Flask app:

```python
import redis
import time
from flask import Flask, jsonify
```

```python
app = Flask(__name__)

# Connect to Redis
cache = redis.StrictRedis(host='localhost',
port=6379, db=0, decode_responses=True)

# Sample data: Simulating a database or external
API call
def get_user_data(user_id):
    # Simulate a delay in fetching data (e.g.,
database or external API call)
    time.sleep(2)
    return {"user_id": user_id, "name": f"User
{user_id}",                         "email":
f"user{user_id}@example.com"}

@app.route('/user/<int:user_id>',
methods=['GET'])
def get_user(user_id):
    # Check if the data is cached in Redis
    cached_data = cache.get(f"user:{user_id}")

    if cached_data:
        print("Cache hit")
        return    jsonify({"source":    "cache",
"data": eval(cached_data)})

    # If data is not cached, fetch it and store
it in Redis
```

```python
    print("Cache miss")
    user_data = get_user_data(user_id)

    # Cache the response for 60 seconds
    cache.setex(f"user:{user_id}",         60,
str(user_data))

    return     jsonify({"source":     "database",
"data": user_data})

if __name__ == '__main__':
    app.run(debug=True)
```

How it works:

- **Redis Connection**: We use the `redis.StrictRedis` client to connect to Redis running on `localhost` (default port 6379).
- **Cache Check**: Before querying the database or simulating a slow API call, we check if the data is already cached in Redis using `cache.get()`.
- **Cache Miss**: If the data is not found in the cache, we fetch it (simulating a database or external API call) and then store it in Redis using `cache.setex()`, with an expiration time of 60 seconds.
- **Cache Hit**: If the data is found in the cache, it is returned directly without making a call to the database or external API.

2. Using Redis for Caching in Express (JavaScript):

To get started, you need to install the **Redis** server and the `redis` Node.js client.

- **Install Redis**: Follow the installation instructions for Redis on your system: https://redis.io/download.
- **Install the Redis Node.js client**:

```bash
bash

npm install redis
```

Here's an example of how to cache API responses using Redis in an Express app:

```javascript
javascript

const express = require('express');
const redis = require('redis');
const app = express();

// Connect to Redis
const client = redis.createClient();

// Sample data: Simulating a database or external
API call
function getUserData(userId) {
  // Simulate a delay in fetching data
```

```
  return new Promise((resolve) => {
    setTimeout(() => {
      resolve({ user_id: userId, name: `User
${userId}`, email: `user${userId}@example.com`
});
    }, 2000);
  });
}


app.get('/user/:userId', async (req, res) => {
  const userId = req.params.userId;

  // Check if the data is cached in Redis
  client.get(`user:${userId}`,      async      (err,
cachedData) => {
    if (cachedData) {
      console.log('Cache hit');
      return res.json({ source: 'cache', data:
JSON.parse(cachedData) });
    }

    console.log('Cache miss');
    const userData = await getUserData(userId);

    // Cache the response for 60 seconds
    client.setex(`user:${userId}`,              60,
JSON.stringify(userData));
```

```
    res.json({    source:    'database',    data:
userData });
  });
});

app.listen(3000, () => {
  console.log('Server          running          on
http://localhost:3000');
});
```

How it works:

- **Redis Connection**: We use the `redis.createClient()` function to connect to Redis.
- **Cache Check**: Before querying the database or making a slow API call, we check if the data is in the Redis cache using `client.get()`.
- **Cache Miss**: If the data is not found in the cache, we simulate fetching it and store it in Redis using `client.setex()`, with an expiration time of 60 seconds.
- **Cache Hit**: If the data is found in the cache, it is returned directly without querying the database or making an API call.

Summary

In this chapter, we learned about **caching** in API development and its benefits in improving performance, reducing server load, and providing faster response times. We covered different caching techniques, including **in-memory caching**, **HTTP caching**, and **database query caching**.

We then saw how to implement caching in your APIs using **Redis**, one of the most popular in-memory data stores, to cache API responses and improve performance. By leveraging caching, you can significantly reduce the number of requests to slow or resource-heavy systems, improving the overall user experience.

In the next chapter, we will dive into **pagination** in APIs, which helps handle large datasets by breaking them into smaller, more manageable chunks.

CHAPTER 15

TESTING YOUR APIS

In this chapter, we will explore how to test your APIs to ensure they work as expected. API testing is crucial for verifying that your endpoints function correctly, handle edge cases, and return the expected responses. We will cover the basics of API testing, using **Postman** for manual testing, and writing **unit tests** for your APIs using **pytest** in Python and **Mocha** in JavaScript.

Introduction to Testing APIs

Testing APIs involves sending requests to the API and verifying that the responses are correct, as well as ensuring that the API behaves as expected in different scenarios. API testing can help you identify bugs, check for performance issues, and ensure that your API adheres to specifications.

There are two main types of testing when working with APIs:

1. **Manual Testing**: Testing APIs by manually sending requests and verifying responses. This is commonly done using tools like Postman.

2. **Automated Testing**: Writing tests in code to verify the behavior of your API. This includes unit tests, integration tests, and end-to-end tests.

139

Testing can be done at different levels:

- **Unit Testing**: Verifies individual components or endpoints.
- **Integration Testing**: Verifies how different parts of your API (e.g., routes, databases) interact.
- **End-to-End Testing**: Verifies the entire API workflow, from receiving a request to sending a response.

Using Postman to Test APIs

Postman is a powerful tool that helps you manually test APIs by sending HTTP requests and inspecting responses. It is widely used for testing, documenting, and interacting with APIs.

Steps to Test APIs with Postman:

1. **Install   Postman**:
   You   can   download   Postman   from
   https://www.postman.com/downloads/.
2. **Creating a Request**:
   o   Open Postman and create a new request by clicking the "New" button and selecting "Request."
   o   Enter the URL of the API endpoint you want to test (e.g., `http://localhost:5000/users`).
   o   Select the HTTP method (GET, POST, PUT, DELETE).

- For POST and PUT requests, you can enter the request body (e.g., JSON data).

3. **Sending the Request**:
   - Click "Send" to send the request to the API.
   - The response will be shown in the Postman interface, including the status code, response body, and headers.

4. **Validating Responses**:
   - You can validate the response by checking the status code (e.g., 200 for success, 404 for not found).
   - Verify the response body contains the correct data. For instance, if you're fetching a user, ensure the user's information matches what's expected.

5. **Adding Tests**: Postman allows you to write test scripts that run after the request. For example, you can write a test to check if the response status is 200 OK:

```javascript
pm.test("Status code is 200", function () {
    pm.response.to.have.status(200);
});
```

Writing Unit Tests for Your API with Python (using `pytest`) and JavaScript (using `Mocha`)

Automated tests are essential for ensuring that your API works as expected, even when changes are made to the codebase. Below, we will cover how to write **unit tests** for APIs in both **Python** and **JavaScript**.

1. Writing Unit Tests in Python using `pytest`

`pytest` is a testing framework for Python that makes it easy to write simple and scalable test cases. You can use `pytest` to test your Flask API endpoints.

Steps for Writing Unit Tests in Python:

1. **Install `pytest`**: To get started, you need to install the `pytest` and `Flask-Testing` libraries:

    bash

    ```
    pip install pytest flask-testing
    ```

2. **Write Tests for Your Flask API**: Here's an example of how to write unit tests for a Flask API using `pytest`:

    Flask API (simple app for testing):

    python

```python
from flask import Flask, jsonify

app = Flask(__name__)

# Sample endpoint
@app.route('/users', methods=['GET'])
def get_users():
    return jsonify({"users": [{"id": 1,
"name": "John Doe"}]}), 200

if __name__ == '__main__':
    app.run(debug=True)
```

Unit Tests for Flask API: Create a file test_app.py for testing your API:

python

```python
import pytest
from app import app  # Assuming your Flask
app is in a file named 'app.py'

@pytest.fixture
def client():
    with app.test_client() as client:
        yield client

def test_get_users(client):
    response = client.get('/users')
```

```
assert response.status_code == 200
assert b'John Doe' in response.data
```

3. **Run Tests**: You can run your tests by executing the following command in your terminal:

```bash
bash
```

```
pytest
```

This will run the test and provide feedback on whether the tests passed or failed.

2. Writing Unit Tests in JavaScript using Mocha

Mocha is a feature-rich JavaScript testing framework that runs on Node.js and in the browser. It is often used in combination with **Chai**, an assertion library, for writing unit tests.

Steps for Writing Unit Tests in JavaScript:

1. **Install Mocha and Chai**: First, you need to install Mocha and Chai in your Node.js project:

```bash
bash
```

```
npm install mocha chai --save-dev
```

144

2. **Write Tests for Your Express API**: Here's an example of how to write unit tests for an Express API using Mocha and Chai:

Express API (simple app for testing):

```javascript
const express = require('express');
const app = express();

app.get('/users', (req, res) => {
  res.json({ users: [{ id: 1, name: 'John Doe' }] });
});

module.exports = app;
```

Unit Tests for Express API: Create a test file, `test/app.test.js`:

```javascript
const chai = require('chai');
const chaiHttp = require('chai-http');
const app = require('../app'); // Assuming your Express app is in a file named 'app.js'
```

145

```
chai.use(chaiHttp);
const { expect } = chai;

describe('GET /users', () => {
  it('should return status 200 and user
data', (done) => {
    chai.request(app)
      .get('/users')
      .end((err, res) => {
        expect(res.status).to.equal(200);

expect(res.body.users[0].name).to.equal('
John Doe');
        done();
      });
  });
});
```

3. **Run Tests**: You can run your tests by executing the following command:

```bash
npx mocha
```

This will run the Mocha tests and provide output on whether the tests passed or failed.

146

Summary

In this chapter, we discussed how to test your APIs using both **manual testing** (with **Postman**) and **automated testing** (using **pytest** in Python and **Mocha** in JavaScript). We covered how Postman allows you to manually test and validate API responses, while `pytest` and Mocha let you write automated unit tests to ensure your API endpoints function as expected.

By integrating automated tests into your development process, you can catch issues early, improve the quality of your code, and ensure that your API continues to work as intended even after changes are made. In the next chapter, we will explore **pagination** in APIs, a technique for handling large datasets efficiently.

CHAPTER 16

API DOCUMENTATION BEST PRACTICES

In this chapter, we will explore the importance of good **API documentation**, best practices for writing clear and effective API documentation, and how to use tools like **Swagger** (now known as **OpenAPI**) to automatically generate interactive API documentation. Clear documentation helps developers understand how to use your API and what to expect from it, making it easier for them to integrate your API into their applications.

Importance of Good API Documentation

API documentation serves as a reference for developers who are integrating or interacting with your API. Good documentation is critical for ensuring that users can easily understand and use your API without confusion. The benefits of good API documentation include:

1. **Improved Developer Experience**: Well-documented APIs make it easier for developers to understand how the API works, reducing the learning curve. It helps them quickly get up to speed and start making requests with minimal effort.

2. **Reduced Support Requests**: Clear and comprehensive API documentation reduces the number of support requests from developers who are confused about how to use the API or unsure of the expected inputs and outputs.

3. **Clear API Expectations**: API documentation defines how the API should behave, what endpoints are available, what parameters are required, and the expected responses. This helps developers know exactly how to interact with the API and what to expect from it.

4. **Consistent Communication**: A consistent format and structure for your documentation ensure that developers can easily find the information they need. It also helps maintain clarity and uniformity across all the API endpoints.

5. **Faster Adoption**: When developers can easily find what they need in your documentation, they're more likely to adopt and integrate your API into their projects.

Tools for API Documentation (Swagger/OpenAPI)

There are several tools available that help you create interactive and standardized API documentation. Two of the most popular tools are **Swagger** and **OpenAPI**.

1. **Swagger (OpenAPI)**: **Swagger** is one of the most widely used tools for creating, documenting, and testing RESTful APIs. Swagger provides an interactive UI for API

documentation, and the **OpenAPI Specification (OAS)** is the standard format used by Swagger to describe APIs.

- o **Swagger UI**: It provides a visual interface for interacting with your API documentation. Users can see all the available endpoints, parameters, and responses, and can try out the API directly from the documentation.
- o **Swagger Editor**: An open-source editor used to create and edit OpenAPI Specification files.
- o **Swagger Codegen**: Automatically generates client libraries, server stubs, and API documentation from an OpenAPI Specification.

2. **OpenAPI Specification (OAS)**: The **OpenAPI Specification** is a language-agnostic standard for describing REST APIs. It is used by tools like Swagger to define the structure of your API. The OpenAPI Specification is written in YAML or JSON format and provides a detailed description of the API, including:

- o Available endpoints
- o Supported HTTP methods (GET, POST, etc.)
- o Parameters and request bodies
- o Responses, including HTTP status codes and response schemas

The OpenAPI Specification helps automate the generation of documentation and client/server code, ensuring consistency across different versions of the API.

3. **Other Documentation Tools**:

    o **Postman**: In addition to being a tool for testing APIs, Postman also provides functionality to generate API documentation. It allows you to generate documentation from your Postman collections.

    o **Redoc**: Redoc is another tool that can generate beautiful and interactive API documentation from OpenAPI specifications. It's often used as an alternative to Swagger UI.

Real-World Example: Documenting Your API with Swagger UI

Let's walk through how you can document your API using **Swagger UI** by defining your API with the **OpenAPI Specification** and using Swagger to generate an interactive documentation interface.

1. Define Your API Using OpenAPI Specification

Here's an example OpenAPI Specification for a simple blog API:

```yaml
openapi: 3.0.0
info:
  title: Blog API
```

```
  description: A simple API for managing blog
posts
  version: 1.0.0
servers:
  - url: http://localhost:5000
paths:
  /posts:
    get:
      summary: Get all blog posts
      operationId: getPosts
      responses:
        '200':
          description: A list of blog posts
          content:
            application/json:
              schema:
                type: array
                items:
                  type: object
                  properties:
                    id:
                      type: integer
                      example: 1
                    title:
                      type: string
                      example: "First Post"
                    content:
                      type: string
```

```
                    example:    "This    is    the
content of the first post."
  /posts/{id}:
    get:
      summary: Get a single blog post by ID
      operationId: getPostById
      parameters:
        - in: path
          name: id
          required: true
          schema:
            type: integer
            example: 1
      responses:
        '200':
          description: The blog post
          content:
            application/json:
              schema:
                type: object
                properties:
                  id:
                    type: integer
                    example: 1
                  title:
                    type: string
                    example: "First Post"
                  content:
                    type: string
```

```
                example:    "This    is    the
content of the first post."
        '404':
          description: Post not found
```

Explanation:

- The `openapi: 3.0.0` line specifies that we are using the OpenAPI 3.0 specification.
- Under the `paths` section, we define two endpoints:
  - `/posts` for retrieving a list of blog posts.
  - `/posts/{id}` for retrieving a single post by its ID.
- Each endpoint has descriptions, expected responses, and parameter definitions (e.g., the `id` parameter for the `/posts/{id}` endpoint).

2. Set Up Swagger UI to Display the Documentation

To use Swagger UI for documenting your API, follow these steps:

1. **Install Swagger UI**: If you're using Flask, you can integrate Swagger UI with **Flask-Swagger-UI**.

   Install the necessary packages:

   bash

   ```bash
   pip install flask-swagger-ui
   ```

2. **Create a Flask App with Swagger UI**:

Here's an example Flask app that serves the Swagger UI documentation:

python

```python
from flask import Flask, jsonify
from         flask_swagger_ui         import
get_swaggerui_blueprint

app = Flask(__name__)

# Set up Swagger UI
SWAGGER_URL = '/swagger'   # URL for the
Swagger UI
API_URL = '/static/swagger.yaml' # Path to
the OpenAPI specification file

swaggerui_blueprint                         =
get_swaggerui_blueprint(
    SWAGGER_URL,
    API_URL,
    config={'app_name': "Blog API"}
)

app.register_blueprint(swaggerui_blueprin
t, url_prefix=SWAGGER_URL)
```

155

```
# Sample endpoint for blog posts
@app.route('/posts')
def get_posts():
    posts = [
        {"id": 1, "title": "First Post",
"content": "This is the first post."},
        {"id": 2, "title": "Second Post",
"content": "This is the second post."}
    ]
    return jsonify(posts)

if __name__ == '__main__':
    app.run(debug=True)
```

Explanation:

- o The get_swaggerui_blueprint function sets up Swagger UI to display your API documentation.

- o The API_URL points to the OpenAPI specification file (swagger.yaml), which should be stored in the /static directory.

- o When you visit /swagger in the browser, Swagger UI will display the interactive API documentation based on the OpenAPI specification.

3. Viewing the Swagger UI: After setting up your Flask app, run it and open your browser at `http://localhost:5000/swagger`. This will display the Swagger UI with interactive documentation that allows you to test the API endpoints directly from the UI.

Summary

In this chapter, we discussed the importance of **good API documentation** and the benefits of using tools like **Swagger** (OpenAPI Specification) to create clear, interactive, and easy-to-understand documentation for your APIs. We explored how to define your API with an OpenAPI specification file, and how to integrate **Swagger UI** into a Flask app to generate interactive documentation.

Good API documentation is key to improving the developer experience, reducing support requests, and promoting the adoption of your API. In the next chapter, we will discuss **API versioning**, a best practice for managing changes to your API over time without breaking existing clients.

CHAPTER 17

BUILDING A RESTFUL API

In this chapter, we will dive into building a **RESTful API** from scratch. We'll start by understanding what makes an API "RESTful," then discuss the core principles of **REST** (Representational State Transfer), and finally, we will create a simple **RESTful API** for managing tasks.

What Makes an API RESTful?

A **RESTful API** is an API that adheres to the principles of **REST (Representational State Transfer)**, which is an architectural style for designing networked applications. REST uses **standard HTTP methods** (GET, POST, PUT, DELETE) and focuses on stateless communication, resource representation, and scalability.

The key features that make an API RESTful are:

1. **Resources**: REST APIs operate around the concept of "resources," which are representations of data that can be manipulated using standard HTTP methods. Resources are typically represented in formats like **JSON** or **XML**.

2. **Stateless Communication**: Every request made to a REST API should contain all the necessary information (including authentication) to complete the request. The

server does not store any state between requests. This makes REST APIs scalable and easier to manage.

3. **Uniform Interface**: A RESTful API should have a consistent and predictable interface, meaning that the way resources are accessed and manipulated should be uniform across the API.

4. **Client-Server Architecture**: In a RESTful system, the client (e.g., web or mobile application) interacts with the server, which is responsible for managing data. The client and server are decoupled, meaning they can evolve independently.

Principles of REST: Statelessness, Cacheability, Layered System

Here are the key principles of REST that guide the design of RESTful APIs:

1. **Statelessness**:
   o Each API request must contain all the information necessary to understand and process the request. The server should not store any state between requests. After a request is completed, no session data should be retained on the server.
   o **Example**: If a client sends a request to fetch a user's profile, the server must authenticate the user with each request. It doesn't rely on any previous session or stored information.

2. **Cacheability**:

- o Responses from the server should be explicitly marked as cacheable or non-cacheable. Cacheable responses can be stored by the client to improve performance, reducing the need for repeated requests to the server.

- o **Example**: A response containing weather data may be cacheable for a certain period, so clients don't need to repeatedly request the same information.

3. **Layered System**:

- o RESTful systems can be composed of multiple layers (e.g., caching layer, application server, database server), each of which performs a specific function. The client doesn't need to know whether it's directly communicating with the final resource server or an intermediary layer.

- o **Example**: In a distributed system, requests might go through a load balancer, caching server, and application server before reaching the database.

4. **Other Principles** (Additional REST Principles):

- o **Uniform Interface**: The interface between clients and servers is uniform and defined by consistent conventions (such as HTTP methods like GET, POST, PUT, DELETE).

o **Representation**: Resources are represented using formats like JSON or XML, which can be transmitted between the client and server.

Real-World Example: Building a Simple RESTful API for Managing Tasks

Let's walk through creating a **RESTful API** for managing tasks. This API will allow users to:

- **Get a list of tasks**
- **Create a new task**
- **Update an existing task**
- **Delete a task**

We will implement this API using **Flask** (Python) and **SQLAlchemy** for database interaction.

1. Install Required Libraries: First, install **Flask** and **SQLAlchemy**:

bash

```
pip install flask flask_sqlalchemy
```

2. Create the Flask App: Here's how you can implement a simple RESTful API in Flask to manage tasks.

python

```python
from flask import Flask, request, jsonify, abort
from flask_sqlalchemy import SQLAlchemy

app = Flask(__name__)
app.config['SQLALCHEMY_DATABASE_URI']         =
'sqlite:///tasks.db'
app.config['SQLALCHEMY_TRACK_MODIFICATIONS']   =
False
db = SQLAlchemy(app)

# Task model
class Task(db.Model):
    id = db.Column(db.Integer, primary_key=True)
    title        =        db.Column(db.String(100),
nullable=False)
    description  =        db.Column(db.String(200),
nullable=True)
    done = db.Column(db.Boolean, default=False)

# Initialize the database
with app.app_context():
    db.create_all()

# GET - Get all tasks
@app.route('/tasks', methods=['GET'])
def get_tasks():
    tasks = Task.query.all()
```

```python
    return jsonify([{'id': task.id, 'title':
task.title, 'description': task.description,
'done': task.done} for task in tasks])

# POST - Create a new task
@app.route('/tasks', methods=['POST'])
def create_task():
    data = request.get_json()
    if not data or not data.get('title'):
        abort(400, description="Title    is
required")

    new_task    =    Task(title=data['title'],
description=data.get('description',           ''),
done=data.get('done', False))
    db.session.add(new_task)
    db.session.commit()

    return jsonify({'id': new_task.id, 'title':
new_task.title,                   'description':
new_task.description, 'done': new_task.done}),
201

# GET - Get a specific task by ID
@app.route('/tasks/<int:id>', methods=['GET'])
def get_task(id):
    task = Task.query.get(id)
    if task is None:
        abort(404, description="Task not found")
```

```python
    return    jsonify({'id':    task.id,    'title':
task.title,    'description':    task.description,
'done': task.done})


# PUT - Update a task
@app.route('/tasks/<int:id>', methods=['PUT'])
def update_task(id):
    task = Task.query.get(id)
    if task is None:
        abort(404, description="Task not found")

    data = request.get_json()
    task.title = data.get('title', task.title)
    task.description  =  data.get('description',
task.description)
    task.done = data.get('done', task.done)
    db.session.commit()


    return    jsonify({'id':    task.id,    'title':
task.title,    'description':    task.description,
'done': task.done})


# DELETE - Delete a task
@app.route('/tasks/<int:id>',
methods=['DELETE'])
def delete_task(id):
    task = Task.query.get(id)
    if task is None:
        abort(404, description="Task not found")
```

```
db.session.delete(task)
db.session.commit()
return jsonify({'message': 'Task deleted'})

# Error handling for 404
@app.errorhandler(404)
def not_found(error):
    return jsonify({'error': 'Not Found',
'message': error.description}), 404

# Error handling for 400
@app.errorhandler(400)
def bad_request(error):
    return jsonify({'error': 'Bad Request',
'message': error.description}), 400

if __name__ == '__main__':
    app.run(debug=True)
```

Explanation of the Code:

- **Task Model**: The `Task` class defines the task structure in the database with fields like `id`, `title`, `description`, and `done`.
- **Database Setup**: We use SQLAlchemy to interact with the database. The `tasks.db` SQLite file stores the tasks.
- **CRUD Operations**:
    - `GET /tasks`: Retrieves all tasks.

165

- o POST /tasks: Creates a new task with a title, optional description, and optional "done" status.
- o GET /tasks/<id>: Retrieves a task by its ID.
- o PUT /tasks/<id>: Updates an existing task by its ID.
- o DELETE /tasks/<id>: Deletes a task by its ID.
- **Error Handling**: The @app.errorhandler() decorator is used to return custom error messages for 404 Not Found and 400 Bad Request.

3. Running the Flask App:

- After writing the code, run the app using:

```bash
```

```
python app.py
```

- The app will be available at http://localhost:5000, and you can interact with the API using tools like **Postman** or **curl**.

Example Requests:

- **GET /tasks**: Fetch all tasks.
- **POST /tasks**: Create a new task.
  - o Example body:

```
json
```

```
{    "title":    "Learn    Flask",
"description":  "Understand  how  to
build APIs with Flask", "done": false
}
```

- **GET /tasks/1**: Retrieve task with ID 1.
- **PUT /tasks/1**: Update task with ID 1.
    - o Example body:

```
json
```

```
{ "done": true }
```

- **DELETE /tasks/1**: Delete task with ID 1.

Summary

In this chapter, we built a **RESTful API** for managing tasks, implementing **CRUD** operations (Create, Read, Update, Delete) for tasks. We followed the **REST principles** to design an API that is **stateless**, uses **standard HTTP methods**, and returns appropriate **status codes** for each operation.

This API can be used as a template for building more complex RESTful APIs for various applications. In the next chapter, we will discuss **API versioning**, a technique for managing changes in your API over time without breaking existing clients.

167

CHAPTER 18

INTRODUCTION TO GRAPHQL

In this chapter, we will introduce **GraphQL**, a powerful alternative to **REST** for building APIs. We will explore the differences between **GraphQL** and **REST**, discuss the advantages of using GraphQL, and walk through a real-world example of building a GraphQL API to fetch blog data.

Understanding the Difference Between REST and GraphQL

Both **REST** and **GraphQL** are approaches for building APIs, but they have significant differences in how they handle data retrieval, structure requests, and manage responses.

REST (Representational State Transfer) APIs are built around fixed endpoints (e.g., `/users`, `/posts`, `/comments`) that return predefined data structures. Each endpoint typically represents a specific resource, and the client makes separate requests to these endpoints to retrieve different pieces of data.

GraphQL, on the other hand, is a query language for APIs that allows the client to request exactly the data it needs, rather than being limited to predefined endpoints. GraphQL enables clients to ask for multiple pieces of related data in a single request, reducing the need for multiple API calls and providing more flexibility.

Here are some key differences between **REST** and **GraphQL**:

1. **Data Fetching**:
   - o **REST**: In REST APIs, you often need to make multiple requests to different endpoints to retrieve related data (e.g., fetching a user, then making another request to fetch the user's posts).
   - o **GraphQL**: In GraphQL, a single request can fetch related data from multiple resources (e.g., a single query can fetch the user and their posts in one request).

2. **Flexibility**:
   - o **REST**: The server defines what data is returned. The client has little control over the response format, often receiving either too much or too little data.
   - o **GraphQL**: The client specifies exactly what data it needs in the query. This results in more efficient responses and avoids over-fetching or under-fetching data.

3. **Versioning**:
   - o **REST**: As your API evolves, changes to the API often require creating new versions (e.g., `/v1/users`, `/v2/users`).
   - o **GraphQL**: GraphQL APIs are versionless. New fields or types can be added to the schema without

breaking existing queries, making it easier to evolve the API over time.

4. **Request Structure**:

   o **REST**: Each request is fixed to a specific endpoint and returns a predefined response structure.

   o **GraphQL**: A single endpoint is used for all requests. The request specifies the shape of the response, and the server returns only the requested data.

Advantages of Using GraphQL

1. **Single Endpoint**:

   o Unlike REST, which typically uses multiple endpoints for different resources, GraphQL uses a single endpoint for all queries and mutations (data changes). This simplifies the API design and makes it easier to manage.

2. **Client-Specified Queries**:

   o GraphQL allows clients to specify exactly what data they need in the request. This means that the server can respond with precisely the required data, reducing the amount of data transferred and improving performance.

3. **Reduced Over-fetching and Under-fetching**:

o In REST APIs, you might get too much data in the response (over-fetching) or not enough (under-fetching). With GraphQL, clients can request only the fields they need, eliminating both over-fetching and under-fetching.

4. **Strongly Typed Schema**:

o GraphQL uses a **schema** to define the structure of the data. The schema is strongly typed, meaning the client and server both know exactly what data types are available and what the query will return. This provides better validation and ensures consistency between the client and server.

5. **Real-time Updates with Subscriptions**:

o GraphQL supports **subscriptions**, which allow clients to subscribe to real-time updates. This is useful for applications that need to display live data, such as chat applications or live feeds.

6. **No Versioning Required**:

o With GraphQL, there's no need for versioning. As your API evolves, you can add new fields and deprecate old ones without breaking existing queries. This reduces the need for complex version management, which is a common challenge in REST APIs.

171

Real-World Example: Building a GraphQL API to Fetch Blog Data

Let's create a simple **GraphQL API** that allows users to fetch blog data, including posts and their associated comments. We will use **Apollo Server** (a popular GraphQL server library) with **Node.js**.

1. Install Dependencies: You need to install the necessary libraries for GraphQL:

bash

```bash
npm init -y
npm install apollo-server graphql
```

2. Define the GraphQL Schema: A GraphQL schema defines the structure of your data and the operations (queries and mutations) that clients can perform. The schema consists of:

- **Types**: Defines the structure of the data.
- **Queries**: Specifies how clients can fetch data.
- **Mutations**: Defines how clients can modify data.

Here's an example of a GraphQL schema for a blog API:

javascript

```javascript
const { ApolloServer, gql } = require('apollo-server');
```

172

```
// Define the GraphQL schema
const typeDefs = gql`
  type Comment {
    id: ID!
    content: String!
    author: String!
  }

  type Post {
    id: ID!
    title: String!
    content: String!
    comments: [Comment]
  }

  type Query {
    posts: [Post]
    post(id: ID!): Post
  }

  type Mutation {
    createPost(title:     String!,     content:
String!): Post
    createComment(postId: ID!, content: String!,
author: String!): Comment
  }
`;
```

```
// Sample data for posts and comments
const posts = [
  {
    id: '1',
    title: 'GraphQL vs REST',
    content: 'GraphQL   is   a   powerful   query
language for APIs.',
    comments: [
      { id: '1', content: 'Great comparison!',
author: 'Alice' },
      { id: '2', content: 'I   prefer   REST,
though.', author: 'Bob' }
    ]
  },
  {
    id: '2',
    title: 'Why Use GraphQL?',
    content: 'GraphQL provides flexibility in API
queries.',
    comments: []
  }
];


// Define resolvers for the queries and mutations
const resolvers = {
  Query: {
    posts: () => posts,
    post: (parent, args) => posts.find(post =>
post.id === args.id)
```

```
  },
  Mutation: {
    createPost: (parent, args) => {
      const newPost = {
        id: String(posts.length + 1),
        title: args.title,
        content: args.content,
        comments: []
      };
      posts.push(newPost);
      return newPost;
    },
    createComment: (parent, args) => {
      const post = posts.find(post => post.id ===
args.postId);
      if (!post) {
        throw new Error('Post not found');
      }
      const newComment = {
        id: String(post.comments.length + 1),
        content: args.content,
        author: args.author
      };
      post.comments.push(newComment);
      return newComment;
    }
  }
};
```

175

```
// Create and start the Apollo Server
const server = new ApolloServer({ typeDefs,
resolvers });

server.listen().then(({ url }) => {
  console.log(`Server ready at ${url}`);
});
```

Explanation:

- **Types**: We define two types: `Post` and `Comment`. Each post can have multiple comments.
- **Queries**:
  - `posts`: Retrieves all blog posts.
  - `post`: Retrieves a single post by its ID.
- **Mutations**:
  - `createPost`: Allows creating a new post with a title and content.
  - `createComment`: Allows adding a comment to a specific post.

3. Run the GraphQL Server: Start the server by running:

```bash
node server.js
```

4. Interact with the API using GraphQL Playground: Once the server is running, visit `http://localhost:4000` to open

GraphQL Playground, an interactive interface for making GraphQL queries and mutations.

Example Queries:

1. **Fetch all posts:**

```graphql
query {
  posts {
    id
    title
    content
    comments {
      id
      content
      author
    }
  }
}
```

2. **Fetch a single post by ID:**

```graphql
query {
  post(id: "1") {
    id
    title
```

177

```
      content
      comments {
        id
        content
        author
      }
    }
  }
```

3. **Create a new post**:

```graphql
graphql

mutation {
  createPost(title: "Learning GraphQL",
content: "GraphQL is a powerful query
language.") {
    id
    title
    content
  }
}
```

4. **Create a new comment**:

```graphql
graphql

mutation {
  createComment(postId: "1", content:
"Great article!", author: "Charlie") {
```

```
        id
        content
        author
    }
  }
```

Summary

In this chapter, we introduced **GraphQL**, a flexible and efficient alternative to REST for building APIs. We discussed the key differences between **REST and GraphQL**, including how GraphQL allows clients to request exactly the data they need. We also explored the advantages of using GraphQL, such as reducing over-fetching and under-fetching of data, supporting real-time updates with subscriptions, and eliminating the need for API versioning.

We then built a simple **GraphQL API** for managing blog data, including posts and comments. The API allows clients to perform **queries** and **mutations** to retrieve and modify blog data. The GraphQL API provides a more efficient way to interact with related resources compared to traditional RESTful APIs.

In the next chapter, we will explore **API versioning** and best practices for managing changes in your API over time without breaking existing clients.

CHAPTER 19

INTEGRATING THIRD-PARTY APIS INTO YOUR WEB APP

In this chapter, we will explore how to **integrate third-party APIs** into your web application. Third-party APIs offer external functionality and data that you can leverage in your own app. We will cover how to use third-party APIs, the common methods for **authentication**, and a real-world example of integrating payment functionality using the **Stripe API**.

How to Use Third-Party APIs (e.g., Google Maps, Twitter, Stripe)

Third-party APIs provide a wide range of services, from data retrieval (e.g., weather, geolocation) to payment processing and social media interactions. Integrating these APIs into your web app can greatly enhance its functionality without the need to build everything from scratch.

The general process for integrating third-party APIs into your web app involves the following steps:

1. **Sign Up and Obtain API Keys**: Most third-party APIs require you to sign up for an account and generate an API key, which is used to authenticate your requests.

2. **Read the API Documentation**: Each API has documentation that explains the available endpoints, authentication methods, rate limits, and response formats.

3. **Make API Requests**: Use HTTP methods (GET, POST, etc.) to interact with the API and retrieve or send data.

4. **Handle Responses and Errors**: Process the data returned by the API and handle any errors that may occur, such as rate limits or invalid requests.

Let's look at some common examples of third-party APIs that you might integrate into your web app:

- **Google Maps API**: Provides functionality for maps, geolocation, and directions.
- **Twitter API**: Allows you to interact with Twitter, post tweets, and fetch user data.
- **Stripe API**: Used to integrate payment processing functionality into your app.

Authentication with Third-Party APIs

When using third-party APIs, **authentication** is a critical step to ensure that only authorized clients can access the API. There are several common methods for authenticating with third-party APIs:

1. **API   Keys**:
   Most APIs require you to pass an API key in the request

header or URL to authenticate your requests. The API key is used to track your usage and ensure that you are authorized to make requests.

- Example (API Key in URL):

bash

```
https://api.example.com/data?api_ke
y=your_api_key
```

2. **OAuth** **2.0**:
Some APIs, especially those involving sensitive user data (e.g., Google, Twitter), use **OAuth 2.0** for authentication. OAuth 2.0 is a protocol that allows users to grant third-party apps limited access to their resources without sharing their login credentials.

- OAuth 2.0 typically involves:
  - Redirecting the user to the authorization server.
  - The user logs in and grants permissions to the app.
  - The app receives an **access token**, which is used to authenticate subsequent requests.

3. **Bearer** **Tokens**:
After authenticating with OAuth, many APIs return a

bearer token that is included in the request header for subsequent requests.

Example:

```bash
```

```
Authorization: Bearer your_access_token
```

Real-World Example: Integrating Payment Functionality with Stripe API

Let's now look at a **real-world example** of integrating a third-party API—specifically the **Stripe API**—into a web app for handling payments. Stripe provides a simple API for accepting payments, managing subscriptions, and more.

Steps to Integrate Stripe API:

1. **Sign Up for a Stripe Account**:
   o Go to Stripe and sign up for an account.
   o After signing up, you will get your **API keys**: one for testing and one for production.
2. **Install Stripe's Node.js SDK**: Stripe provides SDKs for various programming languages. For this example, we'll use the **Node.js SDK**. To install it, run:

```bash
```

```
npm install stripe
```

3. **Create a Payment Form on the Client Side**: Use Stripe's **Stripe.js** library to create a secure payment form on the client side. This will allow users to enter their payment information and send it to Stripe without your server ever handling sensitive data.

HTML (payment form):

html

```
<form id="payment-form">
  <label for="card-element">Credit or
Debit Card</label>
  <div id="card-element"></div>
  <button id="submit">Pay</button>
</form>

<script
src="https://js.stripe.com/v3/"></script>
<script>
  const stripe =
Stripe('your_public_key');
  const elements = stripe.elements();
  const card = elements.create('card');
  card.mount('#card-element');
```

```
const                    form                    =
document.getElementById('payment-form');
   form.addEventListener('submit',      async
(event) => {
      event.preventDefault();

      const {   token,   error   }   =   await
stripe.createToken(card);

      if (error) {
         console.log(error.message);
      } else {
         // Send token to the server
         fetch('/charge', {
            method: 'POST',
            body:    JSON.stringify({   token:
token.id }),
            headers:      {      'Content-Type':
'application/json' },
         });
      }
   });
</script>
```

4. **Handle Payment on the Server Side**: On the server side, use the **Stripe Node.js SDK** to charge the card using the token received from the client.

Node.js (Express server):

185

```javascript

const express = require('express');
const                   stripe                   =
require('stripe')('your_secret_key');
const app = express();
app.use(express.json());

// Handle the payment request
app.post('/charge', async (req, res) => {
  const { token } = req.body;

  try {
    // Create a charge
    const       charge       =       await
stripe.charges.create({
      amount: 5000,   // amount in cents
(e.g., $50.00)
      currency: 'usd',
      description:   'Payment   for   Blog
Post',
      source: token,
    });

    res.status(200).send({ success: true
});
  } catch (error) {
    res.status(500).send({            error:
error.message });
```

```
    }
});

app.listen(3000, () => {
    console.log('Server   is   running   on
http://localhost:3000');
});
```

Explanation:

- o **Client-side**: The user enters their credit card details, and Stripe generates a **token** representing the payment method. This token is sent to the server.
- o **Server-side**: The server uses the **Stripe SDK** to create a charge, passing the token and payment details. If the payment is successful, the server returns a success response.

5. **Test the Payment**:
   - o In your Stripe dashboard, use the **test card numbers** provided by Stripe (e.g., 4242 4242 4242 4242 for a successful test payment) to test the payment flow in development mode.

Summary

In this chapter, we learned how to integrate third-party APIs into your web application. We explored the general process of using

187

third-party APIs, including signing up for API access, authenticating requests, and handling API responses. We then focused on a **real-world example** of integrating a payment solution using the **Stripe API**, which allows you to accept payments, create charges, and manage subscriptions.

By integrating third-party APIs, you can enhance your web applications with powerful features like payment processing, geolocation, social media sharing, and more, without having to reinvent the wheel. In the next chapter, we will discuss best practices for **API versioning**, ensuring that your API can evolve over time without breaking existing clients.

CHAPTER 20

WEBSOCKET APIS AND REAL-TIME DATA

In this chapter, we will explore **WebSockets**, a protocol that enables real-time communication between clients and servers. We'll discuss **what WebSocket is**, **when to use it**, and how to implement WebSocket functionality in **Flask** (Python) and **Express** (JavaScript). Additionally, we will build a **real-time chat application** using WebSocket to demonstrate how it works in practice.

What is WebSocket and When to Use It?

WebSocket is a protocol that provides full-duplex communication channels over a single TCP connection. It is different from traditional HTTP communication, where the client sends a request and the server responds. With WebSocket, both the client and the server can send messages to each other at any time, without having to establish a new connection for each message.

Key Characteristics of WebSocket:

- **Bi-directional communication**: Both the server and client can send messages to each other at any time.
- **Low latency**: WebSocket provides real-time communication with minimal delay.
- **Persistent connection**: Once a WebSocket connection is established, it stays open, allowing for continuous data exchange without needing to repeatedly connect and disconnect.

When to Use WebSocket: WebSocket is best suited for real-time applications where low latency and bidirectional communication are essential. Some common use cases include:

- **Real-time chat applications**: Where users need to send and receive messages instantly.
- **Live notifications**: For real-time updates, such as social media alerts or push notifications.
- **Collaborative tools**: Applications like Google Docs or Trello, where multiple users are working on the same data and need instant synchronization.
- **Live data streaming**: For things like financial data, sports scores, or live news feeds.

WebSocket is particularly useful in scenarios where traditional HTTP requests (with polling or long-polling) would result in high latency or excessive resource consumption.

Implementing WebSocket in Flask and Express

1. **WebSocket in Flask**: Flask does not natively support WebSocket, so we need an additional library, such as **Flask-SocketIO**, to add WebSocket support.

   Installation:

   bash

   ```
   pip install flask-socketio
   ```

   Example: WebSocket in Flask: Here's an example of a simple Flask WebSocket implementation using Flask-SocketIO for a real-time chat application:

   python

   ```
   from flask import Flask, render_template
   from flask_socketio import SocketIO, send

   app = Flask(__name__)
   socketio = SocketIO(app)

   @app.route('/')
   def index():
       return    render_template('index.html')
   # Chat UI (HTML)
   ```

191

```
# WebSocket route to handle real-time
messages
@socketio.on('message')
def handle_message(msg):
    print('Received message: ' + msg)
    send(msg, broadcast=True)  # Broadcast
the message to all clients

if __name__ == '__main__':
    socketio.run(app, debug=True)
```

Explanation:

- o We use `Flask-SocketIO` to enable WebSocket support.
- o The `@socketio.on('message')` decorator listens for incoming WebSocket messages.
- o When a message is received, the server broadcasts it to all connected clients using `send(msg, broadcast=True)`.

HTML (index.html): You'll need a simple front-end to interact with the WebSocket server. Here's a basic example using **JavaScript** and **Socket.IO**:

```html
html

<!DOCTYPE html>
<html lang="en">
```

```
<head>
    <meta charset="UTF-8">
    <meta                    name="viewport"
content="width=device-width,      initial-
scale=1.0">
    <title>WebSocket Chat</title>
    <script
src="https://cdnjs.cloudflare.com/ajax/li
bs/socket.io/4.0.1/socket.io.min.js"></sc
ript>
</head>
<body>
    <h1>Real-Time Chat</h1>
    <ul id="messages"></ul>
    <input  id="message-input"  type="text"
placeholder="Enter message">
    <button
onclick="sendMessage()">Send</button>

    <script>
        const socket = io();

        // Listen for incoming messages
        socket.on('message', function(msg)
{
        const           li          =
document.createElement('li');
        li.textContent = msg;
```

193

```
document.getElementById('messages').appen
dChild(li);
        });

        // Send a message to the server
        function sendMessage() {
            const      message        =
document.getElementById('message-
input').value;
            socket.send(message);   // Send
message to the server

document.getElementById('message-
input').value = '';
        }
    </script>
</body>
</html>
```

Explanation:

- o The `socket.on('message')` listens for messages broadcast by the server and displays them in the `ul` element.

- o The `sendMessage` function sends the message typed by the user to the server using `socket.send()`.

194

2. **WebSocket in Express**: In Express, we use the **ws** library to enable WebSocket functionality.

Installation:

```bash
npm install express ws
```

Example: WebSocket in Express: Here's an example of implementing WebSocket for a real-time chat application in **Express** using the **ws** WebSocket library:

```javascript
const express = require('express');
const WebSocket = require('ws');
const app = express();
const server = app.listen(3000, () => {
    console.log('Server   is   running   on
http://localhost:3000');
});

// Set up WebSocket server
const wss = new WebSocket.Server({ server
});

// Handle WebSocket connections
wss.on('connection', (ws) => {
```

195

```
    console.log('A new client connected');

    // Listen for messages from the client
    ws.on('message', (message) => {
        console.log('Received:      '      +
message);
        // Broadcast the message to all
connected clients
        wss.clients.forEach((client) => {
            if    (client    !==    ws    &&
client.readyState === WebSocket.OPEN) {
                client.send(message);
            }
        });
    });

    // Send a welcome message to the new
client
    ws.send('Welcome to the chat!');
});

app.use(express.static('public'));      //
Serve the front-end from the 'public'
folder
```

Explanation:

o We use the **ws** library to set up a WebSocket server and handle connections.

○ The server listens for incoming WebSocket connections. When a client sends a message, the server broadcasts it to all connected clients.

HTML (public/index.html): The front-end code remains similar to the Flask example, using **JavaScript** to establish a WebSocket connection:

html

```html
<!DOCTYPE html>
<html lang="en">
<head>
    <meta charset="UTF-8">
    <meta                name="viewport"
content="width=device-width,        initial-
scale=1.0">
    <title>Real-Time Chat</title>
</head>
<body>
    <h1>Real-Time Chat</h1>
    <ul id="messages"></ul>
    <input id="message-input" type="text"
placeholder="Enter message">
    <button
onclick="sendMessage()">Send</button>

    <script>
```

```
        const      socket      =        new
WebSocket('ws://localhost:3000');

        // Listen for messages from the
server
        socket.onmessage = (event) => {
            const           li          =
document.createElement('li');
            li.textContent = event.data;

document.getElementById('messages').appen
dChild(li);
        };

        // Send message to the server
        function sendMessage() {
            const         message         =
document.getElementById('message-
input').value;
            socket.send(message);

document.getElementById('message-
input').value = '';
        }
    </script>
</body>
</html>
```

Explanation:

    o The client establishes a WebSocket connection with the server using `new WebSocket('ws://localhost:3000')`.

    o When the client sends a message, it is transmitted to the server using `socket.send()`. The server then broadcasts the message to all other connected clients.

Real-World Example: Real-Time Chat Application Using WebSocket

In this section, we've built a **real-time chat application** using **WebSocket**. Both **Flask (Python)** and **Express (JavaScript)** have been used to implement the server-side WebSocket communication. Clients can send messages to the server, and the server broadcasts these messages to all connected clients in real time.

Key features of this real-time chat application:

- **WebSocket server**: Both Flask and Express handle WebSocket connections and broadcast messages to clients.
- **Client-side communication**: The front-end uses JavaScript to establish a WebSocket connection and send/receive messages.

- **Real-time updates**: Messages are instantly transmitted and displayed without the need for page refreshes.

Summary

In this chapter, we learned about **WebSocket APIs** and how they enable **real-time communication** between clients and servers. We explored the differences between WebSocket and traditional HTTP communication, and we covered the core benefits of using WebSocket for real-time applications. We also built a **real-time chat application** using **WebSocket** in both **Flask (Python)** and **Express (JavaScript)**, demonstrating how WebSocket enables bi-directional communication with low latency.

In the next chapter, we will discuss **API Rate Limiting** and how to prevent misuse or overuse of your API by limiting the number of requests a user can make in a given time period.

CHAPTER 21

DEPLOYING YOUR API TO THE CLOUD

In this chapter, we will explore the process of deploying your API to the cloud. We will provide an overview of popular cloud services like **AWS**, **Heroku**, and **DigitalOcean**, and walk through the steps for deploying both **Flask** (Python) and **Express** (JavaScript) apps to production. Additionally, we will cover a real-world example of deploying an API to **Heroku**, a platform-as-a-service (PaaS) provider.

Overview of Cloud Services: AWS, Heroku, and DigitalOcean

There are many cloud platforms where you can deploy your API. Some are more complex and offer extensive features, while others are simpler and geared towards quick deployments. Let's briefly look at three popular cloud services:

1. **Amazon Web Services (AWS)**: AWS is one of the most widely used cloud platforms and offers a broad range of services including compute power (EC2), storage (S3), and managed services like **AWS Lambda** for serverless computing and **Amazon RDS** for databases.

- o **Use case**: AWS is ideal for building large-scale applications that require high availability, scalability, and flexibility. It is best suited for more complex production environments.
- o **Pros**: High scalability, broad service offerings, global infrastructure.
- o **Cons**: Can be complex for beginners, and pricing can be unpredictable.

2. **Heroku**: Heroku is a **PaaS** (Platform-as-a-Service) that abstracts away most of the infrastructure management. It allows developers to deploy, manage, and scale applications with ease.

- o **Use case**: Heroku is great for small to medium-sized applications, prototypes, or startups that want to get their API live quickly without worrying about infrastructure.
- o **Pros**: Easy to use, great documentation, integrates with many services (e.g., databases, caching, logging).
- o **Cons**: More expensive for larger-scale applications, limited flexibility compared to AWS or DigitalOcean.

3. **DigitalOcean**: DigitalOcean provides cloud computing services similar to AWS but with a focus on simplicity and cost-effectiveness. It offers **droplets** (virtual private servers) that you can configure and manage yourself.

- o **Use case**: DigitalOcean is ideal for small businesses, developers, and startups who want to run their own virtual servers but without the complexity of AWS.
- o **Pros**: Simple and user-friendly interface, lower cost than AWS, good documentation.
- o **Cons**: Less scalability compared to AWS, fewer service options.

Deploying a Flask or Express App to Production

Once you've built your API, the next step is to deploy it to a cloud service so that it is accessible to users. Below, we will walk through the deployment process for both **Flask** (Python) and **Express** (JavaScript) applications.

1. Deploying a Flask App to Heroku

Heroku is one of the easiest platforms for deploying web applications. It abstracts away the underlying infrastructure and allows developers to focus on writing code and deploying apps.

Steps to Deploy a Flask App to Heroku:

1. **Create a Heroku Account**: Sign up for a free Heroku account at https://heroku.com.

2. **Install the Heroku CLI**: Download and install the Heroku CLI to interact with Heroku from the command line. You can download it from here.

3. **Prepare Your Flask App**: Ensure your Flask app is ready for deployment. A typical Flask app has the following structure:

bash

```
/my-flask-app
    ├── app.py
    ├── requirements.txt
    ├── Procfile
    ├── runtime.txt
```

- o **requirements.txt**: List all the dependencies your app needs to run.

  bash

  ```
  flask==2.0.1
  gunicorn==20.1.0
  ```

- o **Procfile**: This file tells Heroku how to run your application.

  bash

  ```
  web: gunicorn app:app
  ```

o **runtime.txt**: Specify the version of Python you want to use on Heroku.

```
python-3.9.6
```

4. **Initialize a Git Repository**: If you haven't already, initialize a Git repository for your app.

```bash
git init
```

5. **Deploy to Heroku**:
   o Log in to Heroku using the Heroku CLI:

```bash
heroku login
```

   o Create a Heroku app:

```bash
heroku create my-flask-app
```

   o Add your remote repository:

```bash
```

```
git       remote       add       heroku
https://git.heroku.com/my-flask-
app.git
```

o   Deploy the app to Heroku:

```
bash
```

```
git add .
git commit -m "Initial commit"
git push heroku master
```

6. **Access Your Flask App**: Once the deployment is complete, you can open your app using:

```
bash
```

```
heroku open
```

Your Flask app is now live on Heroku!

2. Deploying an Express App to Heroku

Deploying an **Express** (Node.js) app to Heroku follows a similar process to Flask.

Steps to Deploy an Express App to Heroku:

1. **Prepare Your Express App**: The structure of an Express app is similar to Flask. Make sure your app has the following files:

bash

```
/my-express-app
    ├── app.js
    ├── package.json
    ├── Procfile
    ├── runtime.txt
```

   o **package.json**: List all dependencies your app needs.

json

```json
{
  "name": "my-express-app",
  "version": "1.0.0",
  "main": "app.js",
  "dependencies": {
    "express": "^4.17.1",
    "dotenv": "^10.0.0"
  },
  "scripts": {
    "start": "node app.js"
  }
}
```

207

- o **Procfile**: Define how to run your app on Heroku.

```
makefile
```

```
web: node app.js
```

- o **runtime.txt**: Specify the version of Node.js.

```
node-14.x
```

2. **Initialize a Git Repository**: Initialize a Git repository for your Express app if you haven't already.

```bash
bash
```

```
git init
```

3. **Deploy to Heroku**:
    - o Log in to Heroku:

    ```bash
    bash
    ```

    ```
    heroku login
    ```

    - o Create a Heroku app:

    ```bash
    bash
    ```

```
heroku create my-express-app
```

o   Add the remote repository:

```
bash
```

```
git    remote    add    heroku
https://git.heroku.com/my-express-
app.git
```

o   Push your app to Heroku:

```
bash
```

```
git add .
git commit -m "Initial commit"
git push heroku master
```

4. **Access Your Express App**: After the deployment is complete, you can open the app with:

```
bash
```

```
heroku open
```

Your Express app is now live on Heroku!

Real-World Example: Deploying an API to Heroku

For this real-world example, we will assume that you have already built a simple **RESTful API** for managing blog posts (similar to the examples we used in earlier chapters).

Steps:

1. Ensure your app is fully functional locally and includes necessary files like `requirements.txt` for Flask or `package.json` for Express.

2. Log in to Heroku via the CLI and create an app.

3. Initialize your Git repository and push your code to Heroku.

4. After deployment, visit the Heroku URL and test your API endpoints.

Example API Endpoints (for Blog API):

- **GET /posts**: Retrieve all blog posts.
- **POST /posts**: Create a new blog post.
- **GET /posts/{id}**: Retrieve a specific blog post by ID.
- **PUT /posts/{id}**: Update a blog post.
- **DELETE /posts/{id}**: Delete a blog post.

Summary

In this chapter, we covered the process of **deploying your API to the cloud** using services like **Heroku**. We explored the differences between popular cloud platforms such as **AWS**, **Heroku**, and **DigitalOcean**, and then walked through the deployment process for both **Flask** and **Express** applications. We also provided a real-world example of deploying an API to Heroku.

Deploying your API to the cloud enables your app to be accessible from anywhere in the world, and cloud services like Heroku make it easy to scale your application as traffic increases. In the next chapter, we will cover **API versioning**, ensuring that your API can evolve over time without breaking existing clients.

CHAPTER 22

VERSIONING YOUR API

In this chapter, we will explore the concept of **API versioning**, why it's essential, and how to implement it in your APIs. We will also discuss the different **versioning techniques** and provide a real-world example of how to add versioning to an existing API.

Why API Versioning is Important

API versioning is the practice of managing changes to your API over time without breaking existing clients. As your API evolves, you may need to add new features, change existing ones, or deprecate certain functionality. Without versioning, these changes could potentially disrupt or break the functionality of clients that rely on the old version of the API.

Key reasons why API versioning is important:

1. **Backward Compatibility**: Versioning allows you to introduce new features and improvements to your API while maintaining backward compatibility. Older clients can continue using the previous version, while new clients can take advantage of the latest changes.

2. **Avoiding Breaking Changes**: APIs need to evolve over time, but certain changes (such as removing an endpoint

212

or changing the structure of a response) may break existing client integrations. Versioning ensures that existing clients are not affected by breaking changes.

3. **Flexibility for Clients**: With versioning, clients can choose to use the version that best fits their needs. For example, a client might not be ready to upgrade to a new version and can continue using an older version of the API without any issues.

4. **Clear Communication**: Versioning provides clear communication about which version of the API a client is using. This allows both the API provider and the consumer to track changes and deprecations over time.

5. **Easier Management of Deprecation**: As APIs grow and evolve, older features may need to be deprecated. Versioning allows for a gradual transition, where old versions can be deprecated over time, giving clients time to migrate to newer versions.

Techniques for Versioning APIs

There are several strategies for versioning APIs. Below are the most common techniques:

1. **URI Versioning**: One of the most common methods of versioning APIs is by including the version in the **URL path**. This makes it clear which version of the API is

being used and allows clients to specify which version they want to interact with.

Example:

bash

```
https://api.example.com/v1/users
https://api.example.com/v2/users
```

- o **Pros**: Easy to understand and implement; clear and explicit.
- o **Cons**: Can lead to URL clutter as more versions are added.

2. **Query Parameter Versioning**: Another approach is to specify the version of the API via a **query parameter** in the URL. This approach keeps the URL cleaner and allows clients to specify the version without changing the URL structure.

Example:

bash

```
https://api.example.com/users?version=1
https://api.example.com/users?version=2
```

- o **Pros**: Clean URLs; easy to implement.

- o **Cons**: Less explicit than URI versioning; it can be harder to track and manage.
3. **Header Versioning**: With header versioning, the version information is passed in the HTTP headers of the request. This approach allows the API URL to remain version-free, and versioning is handled by the HTTP header.

Example:

```bash
```

```
GET /users HTTP/1.1
Host: api.example.com
X-API-Version: 1
```

- o **Pros**: Clean URLs; versioning is separate from the URL.
- o **Cons**: Less discoverable for clients, as they must inspect the headers; not as explicit as other methods.
4. **Accept Header Versioning**: This is a variation of header versioning, where the version information is included in the **Accept** header, typically using a custom MIME type. This method allows you to define multiple versions of the same API, depending on what the client requests.

Example:

```bash
bash
```

```
GET /users HTTP/1.1
Host: api.example.com
Accept: application/vnd.example.v1+json
Accept: application/vnd.example.v2+json
```

- o **Pros**: Clean URLs; versioning is abstracted away in the request header.
- o **Cons**: Can be more complex to implement and manage.

5. **Media Type Versioning**: This method involves specifying the version within the media type of the API response. This is typically done using the `Content-Type` header or custom media type in the request.

Example:

```bash
bash
```

```
Accept: application/vnd.example.v1+json
```

- o **Pros**: No changes to the URL, making it clean and concise.
- o **Cons**: May be less familiar to developers; more complex to implement and track.

Real-World Example: Adding Versioning to an Existing API

Let's assume we have an existing **RESTful API** for managing tasks, and we want to add versioning to support both version 1 and version 2 of the API.

Current API (without versioning):

```python
from flask import Flask, jsonify, request

app = Flask(__name__)

# Sample task data
tasks = [
    {"id": 1, "title": "Learn Flask", "done": False},
    {"id": 2, "title": "Build API", "done": False}
]

@app.route('/tasks', methods=['GET'])
def get_tasks():
    return jsonify(tasks)

@app.route('/tasks', methods=['POST'])
def create_task():
    data = request.get_json()
```

```python
task = {
    "id": len(tasks) + 1,
    "title": data['title'],
    "done": data['done']
}
tasks.append(task)
return jsonify(task), 201


if __name__ == '__main__':
    app.run(debug=True)
```

Steps to Add Versioning (URI Versioning):

1. **Add Version to the URL**: We will modify the endpoints to include the version number in the URL path.

   python

```python
@app.route('/v1/tasks', methods=['GET'])
def get_tasks_v1():
    return jsonify(tasks)


@app.route('/v1/tasks', methods=['POST'])
def create_task_v1():
    data = request.get_json()
    task = {
        "id": len(tasks) + 1,
        "title": data['title'],
        "done": data['done']
    }
```

```
tasks.append(task)
return jsonify(task), 201
```

This adds **version 1** of the API under `/v1/tasks`.

2. **Create Version 2 of the API**: We'll now add version 2 with an updated response format (e.g., including additional fields for task description).

python

```python
@app.route('/v2/tasks', methods=['GET'])
def get_tasks_v2():
    # Version 2 includes an additional
description field for each task
    tasks_v2 = [
        {"id":    task['id'],    "title":
task['title'],    "done":    task['done'],
"description": "No description"}
        for task in tasks
    ]
    return jsonify(tasks_v2)


@app.route('/v2/tasks', methods=['POST'])
def create_task_v2():
    data = request.get_json()
    task = {
        "id": len(tasks) + 1,
        "title": data['title'],
        "done": data['done'],
```

219

```
        "description":
data.get('description', 'No description')
   }
   tasks.append(task)
   return jsonify(task), 201
```

In **version 2** of the API, we introduce a new field `description` for tasks. The structure of the response has been changed to reflect the new field, while still maintaining backward compatibility for clients using version 1.

3. **Handling Deprecation**: If you want to deprecate an old version and guide users to the new version, you can add a **warning header** or include a **deprecation message** in the response.

Example of Deprecation Warning:

```
python
```

```python
@app.route('/tasks', methods=['GET'])
def get_tasks_deprecated():
    response = jsonify(tasks)
    response.headers['Warning'] = '299 -
"This API version is deprecated and will be
removed in the future"'
    return response
```

Testing Versioned API

Once versioning is added, you can test the different versions of the API:

- **GET /v1/tasks**: Fetch tasks using version 1.
- **GET /v2/tasks**: Fetch tasks using version 2 with the additional `description` field.
- **POST /v1/tasks**: Create a task in version 1.
- **POST /v2/tasks**: Create a task in version 2 with the `description` field.

Summary

In this chapter, we explored the concept of **API versioning** and why it is crucial for maintaining backward compatibility and managing changes over time. We discussed various techniques for versioning APIs, including **URI versioning**, **query parameter versioning**, **header versioning**, and **accept header versioning**.

We then provided a real-world example of adding versioning to an existing **Flask API** by introducing version 1 and version 2 of the tasks API. This allows the server to support multiple versions of the API without breaking existing clients.

In the next chapter, we will explore **API security**, including how to authenticate and authorize users for secure access to your API.

CHAPTER 23

SCALING AND OPTIMIZING APIS

In this chapter, we will explore how to **optimize API performance** and **scale your API** to handle increased traffic and provide faster response times. We will discuss various techniques for improving API performance, including **caching**, **load balancing**, and other best practices. Additionally, we will walk through a real-world example of scaling an **eCommerce API**.

How to Optimize API Performance

API performance is crucial for ensuring that your application is responsive, reliable, and scalable. Poor performance can lead to a poor user experience, higher latency, and potentially lost business. Here are some key strategies to optimize your API's performance:

1. **Minimize Response Size**:
   o **Compress Data**: Reduce the size of API responses by using compression techniques like **GZIP**. This can significantly improve performance by reducing the amount of data transferred between the server and the client.
   o **Use Efficient Data Formats**: JSON is commonly used for APIs, but in some cases, other formats

like **Protocol Buffers** or **MessagePack** may offer better performance in terms of speed and size.

2. **Use Asynchronous Processing**:
   - For long-running tasks (e.g., sending emails, processing images), avoid making the client wait for the entire process to finish. Instead, process these tasks asynchronously and notify the client when the operation is complete. You can achieve this by using **message queues** (e.g., **RabbitMQ, Amazon SQS**) or background job processing tools (e.g., **Celery** for Python).

3. **Minimize API Calls**:
   - Reduce the number of requests required to fetch data by combining multiple API calls into a single request (e.g., batch endpoints). This reduces overhead and decreases latency.
   - Use **GraphQL** instead of REST when possible to allow clients to specify exactly what data they need, avoiding over-fetching and under-fetching.

4. **Database Optimization**:
   - Optimize database queries to reduce response times. Use **indexes** for frequently queried fields, optimize join operations, and avoid N+1 query problems.
   - Consider **denormalization** for frequently accessed data to avoid complex joins.

5. **Rate Limiting**:

   o Implement **rate limiting** to control the number of requests clients can make in a given period. This prevents abuse and ensures that resources are not overwhelmed by too many simultaneous requests.

Techniques for Scaling Your API

As your API grows in popularity, it needs to scale to handle an increasing number of users and requests. Here are some common techniques for scaling APIs:

1. **Load Balancing**:

   o Load balancing distributes incoming traffic across multiple server instances to ensure no single server becomes a bottleneck. This improves the reliability and performance of your API by spreading the load evenly.

   o **Types of Load Balancing**:

     ▪ **Round Robin**: Distributes requests evenly to all available servers.

     ▪ **Least Connections**: Routes traffic to the server with the fewest active connections.

     ▪ **IP Hashing**: Routes requests from the same IP address to the same server.

Implementation: Cloud services like **AWS Elastic Load Balancing** (ELB) or **Nginx** can be used to implement load balancing for your API.

2. **Caching**:
   - **Caching** stores frequently accessed data in memory (e.g., **Redis**, **Memcached**) to reduce the need to repeatedly fetch the same data from a database or external service. This significantly reduces response time and decreases the load on backend systems.
   - **Types of Caching**:
     - **Server-side Caching**: Caching API responses on the server to reduce database queries.
     - **Client-side Caching**: Using HTTP caching headers (`Cache-Control`, `ETag`) to store responses on the client side and avoid redundant requests.
     - **Distributed Caching**: Using a caching system like **Redis** or **Memcached** to share cached data between multiple servers.

3. **Horizontal Scaling**:
   - **Horizontal scaling** involves adding more server instances to distribute the load. This is in contrast to **vertical scaling**, which involves upgrading the

server's hardware (e.g., adding more CPU or RAM).

o Horizontal scaling allows you to scale out your API infrastructure to handle increased traffic by adding more nodes or containers.

o Popular tools for container orchestration, such as **Kubernetes**, can help automate horizontal scaling.

4. **API Gateway**:

o An **API Gateway** acts as a reverse proxy, managing requests and routing them to the appropriate backend services. It can provide features like load balancing, caching, authentication, and rate limiting. Popular API gateways include **Amazon API Gateway**, **Kong**, and **Nginx**.

5. **Database Scaling**:

o To scale the database, you can use techniques like **sharding** (splitting the database into smaller parts) and **replication** (creating copies of the database to distribute the load). This can help ensure that the database can handle large numbers of read and write operations.

Real-World Example: Scaling an eCommerce API

Let's walk through how to scale an **eCommerce API** that handles product listings, user management, and order processing.

Scenario: An eCommerce website experiences a surge in traffic during a sale, and we need to scale the API to handle the increased demand.

1. Load Balancing:

- Use a **load balancer** (e.g., **AWS Elastic Load Balancer** or **Nginx**) to distribute incoming requests to multiple server instances. This ensures that no single server is overloaded during the high traffic period.
- Example configuration with **Nginx**:

```nginx
http {
  upstream api_backend {
    server app1.example.com;
    server app2.example.com;
  }

  server {
    location / {
      proxy_pass http://api_backend;
    }
```

227

```
    }
}
```

2. Caching:

- **Product Listings**: Cache the product listings (which don't change often) in a distributed cache like **Redis** or **Memcached**. This reduces the load on the database and improves the response time.

```python
python

import redis

cache                              =
redis.StrictRedis(host='localhost',
port=6379, db=0)

def get_products():
    products = cache.get('products_list')
    if products:
        return products   # Return cached
data
    else:
        # Fetch from database
        products                   =
fetch_products_from_db()
        cache.set('products_list',
products, ex=3600)  # Cache for 1 hour
```

```
return products
```

3. Horizontal Scaling:

- **Backend Servers**: Use **horizontal scaling** to deploy additional application instances in response to increased demand. You can use containerization (e.g., **Docker**) and orchestrate the scaling using tools like **Kubernetes**.
- **Database**: Implement **read replicas** for the database to offload read operations. Use **sharding** to split the database into smaller, manageable chunks.
  - For example, orders placed by users in North America could be stored in a separate shard from users in Europe.

4. API Gateway:

- Use an **API Gateway** to handle incoming requests, manage authentication, and route traffic to the appropriate backend services. An API Gateway can also help manage rate limiting and logging.
- For example, use **Amazon API Gateway** to manage different microservices in the eCommerce application (e.g., user service, product service, order service).

5. Database Scaling:

229

- Use **replication** and **sharding** techniques to scale the database. Replication ensures that read operations are distributed across multiple database instances, while sharding splits the data into smaller chunks that can be processed independently.

- Example: In a product catalog, data related to different categories of products can be stored in separate database shards.

6. Real-Time Features:

- For real-time features like **order status updates** or **live inventory updates**, use **WebSocket** or **Server-Sent Events (SSE)** to push updates to the client immediately.

Summary

In this chapter, we explored how to **scale and optimize APIs** to handle increased traffic and provide faster response times. We discussed **load balancing, caching, horizontal scaling**, and **API gateways** as key techniques for scaling your API. We also covered how to optimize your API for better performance, including minimizing response sizes, using asynchronous processing, and optimizing database queries.

We then applied these techniques to a real-world example of **scaling an eCommerce API**, focusing on ensuring high availability, fast response times, and the ability to handle large volumes of traffic.

In the next chapter, we will dive into **API security**, focusing on best practices for securing your API and protecting sensitive user data.

CHAPTER 24

ADVANCED API TOPICS

In this chapter, we will explore **advanced API topics**, focusing on the concept of **microservices** and how they relate to APIs. We will dive into **API gateways** and their role in microservices architecture, and walk through a **real-world example** of designing a microservice-based API system. These concepts are critical when building large-scale, distributed systems where flexibility, scalability, and resilience are essential.

Introduction to Microservices and APIs

Microservices is an architectural style where an application is developed as a collection of small, independent services, each of which is responsible for a specific piece of functionality. These services communicate with each other over **network protocols** (typically HTTP or message queues) and are often organized around business domains.

In a microservices architecture, each microservice is:

- **Autonomous**: It has its own data store and can operate independently.
- **Deployed independently**: It can be deployed and scaled independently of other services.

- **Communicates via APIs**: Microservices typically expose APIs to interact with each other or external clients. These APIs allow services to send and receive data, process tasks, and communicate asynchronously.

Why Microservices?

- **Scalability**: You can scale individual services based on demand without scaling the entire application.
- **Fault Isolation**: If one microservice fails, the other services can continue to function, improving the resilience of the system.
- **Faster Development and Deployment**: Teams can develop, test, and deploy services independently, speeding up the development cycle.
- **Technology Agnostic**: Different microservices can be written in different programming languages or frameworks, based on the best tool for the job.

APIs in Microservices:

- Each microservice exposes a **set of APIs** that define how other services or clients can interact with it. These APIs serve as the **contract** between services, ensuring communication and data exchange.

- APIs are essential for enabling **loose coupling** between services, meaning that one service can interact with others without needing to know their internal implementation.

API Gateways and Their Role in Microservices

In a microservices architecture, managing communication between multiple services can become complex. An **API Gateway** helps to simplify this by acting as a single entry point for all client requests. It acts as a reverse proxy, routing requests from clients to the appropriate microservice.

Roles of an API Gateway in Microservices:

1. **Routing Requests**:
   - The API Gateway routes incoming client requests to the correct microservice based on the URL path, request type, or other criteria.
   - For example, a request to `/users` might be routed to the User Service, while `/orders` would be routed to the Order Service.

2. **Request Aggregation**:
   - In a microservices setup, a single client request may require responses from multiple services. The API Gateway can aggregate the responses from different services into a single response to send back to the client.

o This helps reduce the number of requests that the client needs to make.

3. **Authentication and Authorization**:
   o The API Gateway can handle authentication and authorization for all microservices, ensuring that only authorized users can access the services. This centralizes security and reduces the complexity of each microservice needing to manage it independently.
   o It can validate **JWT tokens** or other types of authentication headers before routing requests.

4. **Load Balancing**:
   o API Gateways can distribute traffic evenly across multiple instances of microservices to prevent any single instance from being overwhelmed.

5. **Rate Limiting**:
   o The API Gateway can manage rate limiting, ensuring that clients do not overload the services by making too many requests in a short period.

6. **Logging and Monitoring**:
   o The API Gateway can log and monitor requests to provide insights into API usage and performance across microservices. This helps with debugging and performance tuning.

7. **Cross-cutting Concerns**:

o The API Gateway can handle other cross-cutting concerns such as caching, request/response transformation, and error handling.

Popular API Gateway Solutions:

- **Kong**: An open-source API Gateway that can handle load balancing, security, and rate limiting.
- **Nginx**: A popular reverse proxy that can be used as an API Gateway.
- **Amazon API Gateway**: A fully managed service that handles API routing, security, and scaling in AWS environments.
- **Apigee**: A Google-owned API management solution that provides features for API routing, security, and analytics.

Real-World Example: Designing a Microservice-Based API System

Let's design a microservice-based system for an **eCommerce application** that includes services like **User Service**, **Product Service**, and **Order Service**. We will also incorporate an API Gateway to manage the communication between services and handle incoming client requests.

1. Define the Microservices:

- **User Service**: Manages user authentication, profiles, and account management.

236

- o Endpoints:
  - POST /users/signup: Create a new user.
  - POST /users/login: Log in a user and return a JWT token.
  - GET /users/{id}: Retrieve user details by ID.
- **Product Service**: Manages the products in the catalog.
  - o Endpoints:
    - GET /products: Get a list of products.
    - GET /products/{id}: Get details of a specific product.
    - POST /products: Add a new product (Admin-only endpoint).
- **Order Service**: Manages customer orders.
  - o Endpoints:
    - POST /orders: Create a new order.
    - GET /orders/{id}: Get order details by ID.
    - GET /orders/user/{userId}: Get all orders for a specific user.

2. Define the API Gateway: The API Gateway will expose a single endpoint for all client requests. It will handle routing to the appropriate microservices and manage authentication.

API Gateway Routes:

- POST /api/login: **Routes to** POST /users/login in the User Service.
- GET /api/products: **Routes to** GET /products in the Product Service.
- POST /api/orders: **Routes to** POST /orders in the Order Service.

API Gateway Responsibilities:

- **Authentication**: The API Gateway verifies the user's JWT token for protected routes like creating an order.
- **Rate Limiting**: The API Gateway applies rate limits to prevent abuse.
- **Routing**: The API Gateway routes requests to the appropriate microservice (User Service, Product Service, or Order Service).
- **Logging**: The API Gateway logs all incoming requests for auditing and debugging purposes.

3. Implementing the API Gateway: We will use **Nginx** as the API Gateway in this example. Here's how we can configure Nginx to route requests to different microservices:

Nginx Configuration (nginx.conf):

```nginx

http {
```

```
upstream user_service {
    server user-service:5000;
}

upstream product_service {
    server product-service:5001;
}

upstream order_service {
    server order-service:5002;
}

server {
    listen 80;

    # Route /api/login to the User Service
    location /api/login {
        proxy_pass http://user_service;
    }

    # Route /api/products to the Product
Service
    location /api/products {
        proxy_pass http://product_service;
    }

    # Route /api/orders to the Order Service
    location /api/orders {
        proxy_pass http://order_service;
```

```
            }
        }
    }
```

Explanation:

- **Upstreams**: We define upstreams for each microservice (User Service, Product Service, and Order Service) that specify where requests should be routed.
- **Routing**: We configure Nginx to route requests for `/api/login` to the **User Service**, `/api/products` to the **Product Service**, and `/api/orders` to the **Order Service**.

4. Microservices and API Gateway Communication: Each microservice (e.g., User Service, Product Service, and Order Service) runs as an independent service in Docker containers or virtual machines, with Nginx routing requests to the appropriate service based on the URL path.

5. Scalability: To scale the system, we can deploy multiple instances of each microservice and load balance the requests across those instances using Nginx or another load balancer. The API Gateway (Nginx) will handle the traffic and distribute it evenly across the services.

Summary

In this chapter, we explored **microservices** architecture and how APIs play a key role in enabling communication between independent services. We discussed the role of the **API Gateway** in microservices, including routing requests, handling authentication, and providing other cross-cutting concerns like rate limiting and logging.

We also walked through a **real-world example** of designing a microservice-based API system for an eCommerce application. The system consisted of services for managing users, products, and orders, with an API Gateway acting as the central point of entry for clients.

Microservices and API Gateways help create scalable, flexible, and resilient systems, allowing for easier development, testing, and deployment of individual services. In the next chapter, we will discuss **API monitoring and analytics**, focusing on how to track the performance and usage of your API in production.

www.ingramcontent.com/pod-product-compliance
Lightning Source LLC
LaVergne TN
LVHW022340060326
832902LV00022B/4144